FINDING GOD BEYOND THE CHURCH

A MYSTICAL JOURNEY INTO AUTHENTIC SPIRITUALITY

HAROLD G. BIRKENHEAD

APOCRYPHILE PRESS

Apocryphile Press
PO Box 255
Hannacroix, NY 12087
www.apocryphilepress.com

Copyright © 2025 by Harold G. Birkenhead
Printed in the United States of America
ISBN 978-1-965646-37-3 | paper
ISBN 978-1-965646-38-0 | ePub

No part of this book may be reproduced, stored in a retrieval system, or transmitted in any form or by any means—electronic, mechanical, photocopy, recording, or otherwise—without written permission of the author and publisher, except for brief quotations in printed reviews.

The author would like to thank Janeen Jones for her excellent editing.

Please join our mailing list at www.apocryphilepress.com/free. We'll keep you up-to-date on all our new releases, and we'll also send you a FREE BOOK. Visit us today!

*For my precious wife, Charlene, and our children
—Chris, Caroline, Emma, and Tim—
through whom I came to see God
in the life we lived together.*

CONTENTS

Introduction   vii

PART ONE
THE CHURCH WE KNEW, THE FAITH WE'RE FINDING

1. Jesus Never Came to Establish a Church   3
2. The Veil That Was Never Meant to Stay   9
3. The Mystical Jesus   14
4. Spirituality Beyond the Church   28
5. Releasing Guilt   34
6. A Call to Something More   40

PART TWO
PRACTICES FOR A LIVING FAITH

7. How Do I Find God Beyond the Church?   51
8. The Listening Life   56
9. A Spirituality of Companionship   62
10. Beyond the Walls   68

PART THREE
WALKING THE PATH WITH DEPTH AND COURAGE

11. The Inner Self as Teacher   75
12. Pilgrimage of the Soul   80
13. Letting Go of Certainty   85
14. Thin Places and Timeless Moments   90
15. Companions on the Road   93

PART FOUR
BLESSINGS AND PRACTICES FOR THE JOURNEY

Final Word   99
Practices for the Journey   101
The Mystical Toolbox   104

INTRODUCTION
LONG AGO AND FAR AWAY

There was a time when the Church was home. It held beauty, order, and meaning. It echoed with the music of the soul and lifted prayers like incense to the heavens. I gave my life to it—for decades I preached, prayed, counseled, and baptized under its vaulted arches. But over time, the voice that once sang clearly through its liturgy grew faint beneath the weight of politics, bureaucracy, and agendas far removed from Spirit.

The Church, as we once knew it, is dying. Not because people have lost their longing for God, but because many no longer find God within its walls. After decades in ministry and a lifetime of devotion, I find myself echoing what so many quietly feel: the institution that once nourished our souls has strayed far from its calling. What began as a spiritual movement centered on love, transformation, and unity has, over time, become entangled in politics, business models, and power structures that often seem more interested in survival than salvation.

If you're anything like me and have lived long enough to remember the days when church life was at the heart of American society, you'll recall a time when mainline churches were alive with excitement, vitality, and a deep sense of spirituality. I was raised in the Episcopal Church, a sacred space where warmth, mystery, and beauty filled the air. It was a place where the music soared, the prayers seemed to reach beyond the heavens, and the community gathered with hearts full of reverence. The presence of God was tangible in the silence of candlelit chapels, in the soft flicker of altar lights, and in the harmonies of the choir. For me, this was the essence of worship —a rich, immersive experience that made the divine feel as real and present as the air we breathe.

This was the late 1950s, often referred to as a golden age for organized religion. Churches were thriving, expanding, and filling the pews to accommodate a growing population. Faith was a cornerstone of American life, woven into the fabric of society. Between 1955 and 1958, nearly half of all Americans attended church each Sunday—the highest percentage in U.S. history. The Episcopal Church, in particular, flourished, growing faster than the population and drawing many who sought spiritual nourishment and guidance.

But something shifted. By the mid-to-late 1960s, the winds of change began to blow. The tumultuous years of the Vietnam War brought uncertainty, disillusionment, and a deep reevaluation of societal institutions, including the Church. As the world began to question the status quo, church membership growth slowed dramatically. What had once been a steady increase dwindled. By 1967, the Episcopal Church had lost more than 62,000 members. Like so many other denominations, the wellspring of spiritual vitality that had once defined the Church began to dry up, replaced by an emphasis on politics, bureaucracy, and institutional survival.

This decline only continued. Today, the Episcopal Church has seen a reduction of more than half its membership, shrinking from around 3.8 million in 1966 to just 1.55 million in 2023. This pattern is not unique to one denomination. Across the Christian world, churches have closed their doors, congregations have dwindled, and many ministries now operate on a part-time basis. A troubling study by the Barna Group revealed that between 2000 and 2020, the number of practicing Christians in the U.S. nearly halved. Meanwhile, a Gallup poll found that for the first time in eight decades, U.S. church membership had fallen below 50%.

But is this truly a sign of Christianity's collapse—or is it, perhaps, a sign that institutional churches, as they are currently structured, have become outdated and irrelevant?

For too long, church leaders have responded to this decline with bureaucratic solutions—forming committees, writing reports, and trying to revive fading programs—without ever addressing the core issue. The real question is not how to bring people back into church, but why so many have left in the first place. When church leaders do hear the voices of the people, they often dismiss their concerns, labeling them as unimportant. A 2017 survey by Lifeway Research found that 66% of Americans aged 23–30 stopped attending church for at least a year after turning 18. Their reasons? They saw the Church as divisive, judgmental, and hypocritical.

The COVID-19 pandemic didn't cause this decline; it merely exposed what was already unraveling. For me, however, the unraveling began long before the pandemic.

This awareness became even more apparent after my wife, Charlene, passed away. In the depths of grief, I turned to the Diocese I had served for so long, expecting comfort and solace. Instead, I was met with silence. The institution I had given so much to had nothing to offer me in my darkest hour. It was in that silence that I discovered something profound: God was never confined to a building, a ritual, or an organization. The divine had always been with me, within me, and around me, speaking in ways I hadn't yet understood.

And yet... the journey did not end when I stepped beyond its walls. In fact, that's where the real journey began.

This book is not about abandoning faith. It is about deepening it—about rediscovering a direct and personal experience of God that institutional religion too often obscures. What I found beyond the Church was not exile but invitation. Not a void but a Presence. A call to walk the mystical path—a path available to all, not just monks and mystics, but everyday people hungry for something more.

At its heart, mysticism is simply the experience of union with the Divine. It is not a system or creed but a relationship. It does not require robes or rituals, though it can live within them. It requires only a willing heart, an open mind, and the courage to listen for the voice of God within your own soul.

This is not a solitary path, though it is deeply personal. Along the way, I've found companions in conversation, in silence, in nature, and in unexpected communities that gather around shared longing rather than shared dogma. Together, we are building something new—not a traditional church, but sacred spaces for authenticity, connection, and Presence.

In the pages that follow, I'll reflect on what I've lost and what I've found. I'll share practices that help me listen—prayer, meditation, dreamwork, and contemplation—and stories from those who walk similar paths. This is a book for the seekers, the disillusioned, the quietly faithful. For those who have not lost Their Faith, but are finding it in a different way.

The road ahead is not always clear. But it is holy.

Let's walk together.

PART ONE
THE CHURCH WE KNEW, THE FAITH WE'RE FINDING

"You cannot put new wine into old wineskins."
—Matthew 9:17

Before we can fully imagine a faith beyond the Church, we must reckon with the Church we've known—its beauty, its failures, and its fading presence in the lives of so many.

This part of the book is not a theological takedown, but a personal excavation. These chapters reflect on the sacred memories that once drew us in, the shifts that led us to question, and the grief that often accompanies letting go.

It is also about honoring the soul's refusal to settle. Many of us didn't walk away from the Church—we were quietly pushed out by politics, neglect, or spiritual dryness. And yet, our longing for the Divine persisted.

Let this part be a mirror. You may see your own story here, or find language for something you've felt but never named. Either way, this is where the journey begins.

CHAPTER 1
JESUS NEVER CAME TO ESTABLISH A CHURCH

Is it true that Jesus never came to establish a church?

Before we can embark on a journey of discovering God beyond the boundaries of organized religion, this question must be addressed honestly. If we are to find a spiritual path outside the Church, we need assurance that such a pursuit is not only valid but also biblically and theologically supported, especially when viewed through a mystical or non-institutional lens.

The answer is yes. Jesus did not come to establish a Church, a new religion, or reform the old. He came to awaken hearts and guide us back to our Father, calling us not into hierarchy, but into divine relationship.

Jesus walked dusty roads, not marble aisles. He taught on hillsides and shorelines, not from pulpits. His life was immersed in Spirit, shaped by silence, solitude, and the deep inner knowing that comes not from doctrine, but from union. Jesus was, at heart, a mystic.

He offered no blueprints for buildings or manuals for institutional governance. Instead, he told parables—mystical stories layered with meaning, not designed to define but to awaken. "The kingdom of God is within you," he said—not within walls or systems but in the quiet, inner place where Spirit whispers.

He often withdrew from the crowds to pray alone, not to escape, but to return. These moments of solitude weren't merely pauses between public ministry—they were its source. In the stillness of the desert and the hush of the mountain, he communed with the Father—not as a distant deity, but as the very presence of love within and around him.

At the core of his teaching was a radical truth: God is not distant, but alive within us. Jesus did not come to place a religious institution between us and the Divine. He invited each person into a living relationship with the Holy—marked by love, humility, and awakening. "The Kingdom of God is within you" (Luke 17:21). This wasn't about ritual or dogma; it was about divine presence.

Jesus walked among the people. He healed, shared meals, and uplifted those forgotten by society. He wore no robes of authority and kept no distance from the ordinary. He spoke to fishermen, tax collectors, women, and outcasts, revealing that the sacred is found in compassion, connection, and everyday moments. The true temple, he taught, is the open, seeking heart.

The Kingdom he proclaimed was not a future empire but a present reality—here and now, available to all. It was an invitation to return to harmony with the Creator, beyond ego, division, and sin—a kingdom of love, unity, and inner transformation.

Jesus frequently challenged religious institutions. He condemned hypocrisy and the use of religion for power and control. He overturned tables in the temple (Matthew 21:12) and rebuked those who upheld tradition but ignored compassion.

To Jesus, God's dwelling was not in brick and stone but in the hearts of those who seek with sincerity. Even his death—so often interpreted as transactional atonement—carried a more profound meaning: the breaking of spiritual chains.

"Blessed are the pure in heart, for they shall see God" (Matthew 5:8). This was not a call to external conformity but to inner transformation.

This message—that the Divine resides within—echoed beyond Jesus' own words. The early followers, including Paul, carried this vision forward. Though Paul later became instrumental in shaping early Church structures, at his best he reinforced Jesus' spiritual message: "Do you not know that your body is a temple of the Holy Spirit within you?" (1 Corinthians 6:19). The sacred was not confined to any building or priesthood, but alive in each seeker's heart.

Seen through this lens, it becomes clear: Jesus' mission was never to found a hierarchical institution. He came to ignite the Divine spark in each soul and restore our origin and destiny—union with the Father.

To follow Jesus is to enter into this same mystical rhythm, not of rules and rituals, but of inner listening and divine encounter. He invited others not to worship him, but to follow him into the mystery of oneness. He didn't start a religion; he opened a way.

The Church, as we know it, formed generations later, long after Jesus had already planted the seeds of the kingdom within hearts, not hierarchies. His original message—radical, intimate, and spiritually liberating—was never meant to be institutionalized. It was meant to be lived.

BIBLICAL VALIDATION

The Bible clearly speaks to those who seek scriptural assurance that this path is not only possible but also true to Jesus' teachings.

JESUS FOCUSED ON RELATIONSHIP, NOT STRUCTURE

> "I am the way, the truth, and the life. No one comes to the Father except through me." —John 14:6

This wasn't a statement of exclusivity, but an invitation into awakened being—into the Divine "I AM" that reconnects us with God.

> "Now this is eternal life: that they know you, the only true God, and Jesus Christ, whom you have sent." —John 17:3

Eternal life is found not through institutional membership but through relationship.

THE KINGDOM OF GOD WAS CENTRAL

Jesus spoke of the Kingdom more than a hundred times, never of founding a Church. His metaphors—mustard seed, leaven, hidden treasure—spoke of something small, intimate, and internal.

> "The kingdom of God does not come with observation...for indeed, the kingdom of God is within you." —Luke 17:20-21

> "I am in the Father, and you in me, and I in you." —John 14:20

These are mystical teachings of union, not calls for religious separation or superiority.

JESUS CHALLENGED RELIGIOUS INSTITUTIONS

> "Woe to you, scribes and Pharisees, hypocrites!" —Matthew 23

He exposed the danger of religion without Spirit when law eclipses love.

EARLY CHRISTIANITY WAS A MOVEMENT, NOT A CHURCH

The earliest followers were called Followers of the Way (Acts 9:2; Acts 24:14). The Greek word often translated as "church" (ecclesia) meant an assembly or gathering, not a religious institution.

Christianity became formalized under Emperor Constantine and the Council of Nicaea in 325 AD—three centuries after Jesus. Paul and others helped structure Christian communities, introducing roles such as bishops and elders for survival, not as divine blueprints but as practical solutions to the growing challenges.

IN SUMMARY

Jesus never came to establish a Church. His mission was spiritual, not institutional. He came to reveal the Kingdom of God within, to restore our direct connection with the Divine, and to call us into lives of love, compassion, and awakening. The Church that followed was a human response, not a divine mandate.

Seeking God beyond the Church is not a betrayal of Jesus—it is a return to his original invitation: to find God within.

And if Jesus' mission was not to build an institution but to awaken the soul, then perhaps our spiritual search today can be just as vibrant when we look beyond the walls, into the wonder of our inner life and the sacred woven through each moment.

Many have walked away from the Church not because they've lost faith, but because they seek something deeper—

something real. What if the walls that once protected the sacred have now become barriers to it? What if the mystery of God was never meant to be hidden behind stained glass and doctrine?

In the next chapter, we'll explore the ancient symbol of the veil—a veil meant to fall away. For centuries, religion has kept it intact, yet it is this very veil that must be lifted to encounter the living presence of God already within and among us.

AFFIRMATION

> *I walk in the footsteps of the Teacher,*
> *not toward a steeple, but into the sacred heart of life.*
> *The Spirit is not confined—*
> *it breathes in me, beyond walls and beyond fear.*
> *I am free to seek, free to find,*
> *and free to follow the living Christ within.*

CHAPTER 2
THE VEIL THAT WAS NEVER MEANT TO STAY

What Is the Veil?

Throughout spiritual history, the veil has symbolized the boundary between the seen and unseen, the sacred and the profane, the human and the Divine. Ancient religious traditions used veils to signify the divine mystery. In ancient Egyptian rites, veils were draped over the statues of the gods, only to be lifted during certain rituals. In Greek mystery religions, the unveiling represented a revelation of divine truth to the initiate.

In ancient Hebrew tradition, the veil in the Temple separated the Holy of Holies, where God's presence was believed to dwell, from the rest of the sanctuary. Only the High Priest could pass through this veil once a year on the Day of Atonement. It was not just a physical barrier but a spiritual one, representing humanity's sense of distance from God.

In Christian thought, this image is transformed at the moment of Jesus' death. The Gospels tell us that the veil of the Temple was torn from top to bottom (Matthew 27:51). This powerful image has been interpreted as the end of the separation between God and humanity. What once kept us out is now open. The Holy is no longer confined to a sanctuary—God is within us.

Mystical traditions across cultures echo this theme. The veil is the illusion that God is distant or inaccessible. It represents the layers of perception, belief, and ego that keep us from direct experience of the Divine. In the East, it is called maya, the illusion of separateness. In mystical Christianity, it is the false self, the ego, or the conditioned mind. Yet in every tradition, the veil is not meant to be permanent. It is a threshold—a necessary protection until the soul is ready to see.

THE PURPOSE OF THE VEIL

The veil serves a spiritual function. It prepares us and invites us into the mystery. Much like a curtain before a stage, it conceals until the soul is mature enough to witness the truth behind it. In this way, the veil fosters a yearning—a hunger for something more, a revelation. That revelation is the beginning of the mystical path.

The veil teaches us that faith must evolve into knowing. Belief systems may bring comfort, but they are not substitutes for experience. When we are ready, the veil is lifted not by effort but by grace, often in moments of deep prayer, meditation, grief, or love. These are the cracks through which the light enters. These experiences invite us beyond the known and into the sacred.

Jesus, as a mystic teacher, understood this. He often spoke in parables—stories layered with meaning. To the casual listener, they were riddles. But to those with awakened hearts, they were invitations to see beyond the surface. "He who has ears to hear, let him hear," he would say. He knew that truth could not be forced. It must arise within, recognized by the soul, not imposed by doctrine.

The parables, like the veil itself, pointed toward a deeper reality. They bypassed the intellect and stirred the heart. Jesus' words were keys, unlocking inner doors. He spoke this way not to hide the truth, but to let it emerge in those ready to perceive it.

THE CHURCH AS VEIL

Over time, the institutional Church has become, for some, another veil. What was meant to guide us into the mystery of God has sometimes become the very thing that obscures it. In its quest for structure and certainty, the Church has often replaced spiritual experience with doctrine, mystery with dogma, the living Christ with a static image.

Rather than revealing God, it can anchor us to intermediaries. Rather than stirring awe, it can settle for certainty. Rather than opening us to the sacred within, it can direct our attention only to the authority without. And yet, just like the Temple veil, the Church was never meant to stay in place forever. It was never meant to stand between us and God.

The journey beyond the Church is not an abandonment of faith, but a return to it. It is the same journey mystics have always taken. It is the path of awakening—the sacred search to experience God directly, intimately, without veil or mediator. It is not rebellion; it is remembering.

PIERCING THE VEIL

When the veil is lifted—whether through loss, love, silence, or joy—we realize something extraordinary: we were never truly separated. God was never absent. The Divine was not hiding in heaven or behind ecclesiastical walls. The presence of God has always been here, closer than breath, waiting to be known.

When we pray with our hearts open, when we meditate and

listen deeply, when we walk through grief and come out changed, the veil begins to thin. We may dream of loved ones or receive insight from within. We may find peace in nature or sudden clarity in silence. These are not fantasies—they are glimpses beyond the veil.

The great truth revealed is this: the kingdom of God is not out there. It is within us. As Jesus said, "The kingdom of God is within you" (Luke 17:21). The mystical path does not lead us away from life but deeper into it. It teaches us to see the sacred in all things and to find the extraordinary in the ordinary.

LIFE AS THE VEIL

However, the veil is not only in temples, traditions, or religious systems. The veil is life itself—at least, life as we often live it. The busyness of our days, the distractions of the world, the wounds we carry, and the personas we adopt can all veil our awareness of the Divine presence that is always here.

We are born into a world that teaches us separation. From the first breath, we are given names, identities, roles, and expectations. We learn what is sacred and what is not. We learn what is permitted and what is punished. Slowly, layer by layer, the veil forms—not maliciously, but protectively, as the soul finds its footing in this world of form.

This veil of ordinary life is necessary in its time. We must grow, stumble, question, and search. We must suffer the ache of longing to recognize the fullness of union. But the true self—the spark of God within us—never forgets. It calls to us through beauty, pain, and moments of stillness. It whispers that there is more, that we are more.

The mystic path is not about escaping life but seeing through it. It is about realizing that life, even its veils, can become portals. Every grief, joy, relationship, and challenge can become a place of awakening if we are willing to look with spiritual eyes.

So when you feel far from God, don't ask, "Where is God?"—ask instead, "What veil am I wearing?" Is it fear? Guilt? Shame? Pride? Whatever it may be, only you can remove the veil. Sometimes, even the Church itself—or your own ideas of what spirituality should look like—can become veils, obscuring the presence of the Divine.

Living with spiritual awareness doesn't take you to another realm—it opens your eyes to the one you're already in. This is the sacred paradox: the veil was never meant to stay, yet it served its purpose. It shielded us until we could bear the light. It awakened the longing of the soul so we might seek the Beloved. Now, the seeking becomes seeing.

This journey you are taking, dear reader, is not only appropriate but holy. You are not alone. You are walking the path of those who, throughout time, have dared to believe that the veil was never meant to stay.

When the veil is lifted, the view begins to change. What—or who—do we see more clearly on the other side? When the veil begins to lift, we are left with a crucial question: who was Jesus really trying to show us? Beneath layers of religious interpretation and centuries of theology lies a mystic—a teacher of inner truth, oneness, and love. Having explored the sacredness of interior transformation and personal connection to the Divine, we now turn to the life of one who embodied this fully: Jesus the Mystic.

AFFIRMATION

The veil has lifted.
I see with the eyes of my soul.
God is not distant—I am one with the Divine, here and now.

CHAPTER 3
THE MYSTICAL JESUS

INTRODUCTION: SEEING JESUS AS A MYSTIC

Jesus of Nazareth is often portrayed primarily as Teacher, Prophet, and Savior—roles he undoubtedly embodied. Yet beneath these titles lies a deeper identity: that of a mystic who walked the contemplative path with profound intimacy.

A mystic doesn't simply speak of spiritual truths, but lives them—piercing the veil of ordinary perception to dwell in the hidden realm of unity and divine presence. In this chapter, we will explore how Jesus' life and teachings exemplify the mystical journey, offering a blueprint for all who yearn to know God directly.

From the beginning of his ministry, Jesus modeled contemplative practices that transcended religious form. He withdrew into solitude to pray in the wilderness—not to escape people, but to commune with the Father in silence. He spoke in parables—stories that bypassed the conscious mind and invited listeners into inner transformation. Through his "I Am" declarations, he revealed his unbroken union with the Divine, not pointing to a distant heaven, but to a living presence within every soul.

By studying Jesus as a mystic, we learn that the spiritual life is not about accumulating beliefs or adhering to rituals alone. It is about cultivating a moment-by-moment awareness of God's nearness. Jesus' very being radiated this awareness: in his compassion, in his fearless healing, and in his gracious acceptance of all. His life pierced the veil of separation, declaring that the Kingdom of God is not somewhere else but already here, already within us.

In the pages that follow, we will trace the key elements of Jesus' mystical path—his use of silence and solitude, his teaching through parables, his demonstrations of union consciousness, and the symbolic depth of his miracles. Each serves as an invitation—not merely to admire Jesus' mysticism, but to follow in his footsteps, awakening our own capacity to know God directly. Let us begin by stepping into the sacred atmosphere he created, learning to see through the veil and abide in the ever-present mystery of the Divine.

PARABLES AS KEYS TO THE INNER KINGDOM

Jesus often chose parables over direct teaching because stories speak to the heart in ways that doctrine alone cannot. Parables bypass the analytical mind and open a "door" directly into contemplative insight. They invite the listener to lean in—not to analyze, but to sense the truth unfolding within, and to discover the kingdom hidden in plain sight.

There were prominent reasons why Jesus spoke in parables rather than preaching lectures. First, he wanted to activate his listeners' imaginations. A story stirs the imagination, engaging the whole person—mind, body, and spirit—in a unifying experience of truth. Second, to give individual revelation. Parables allow each listener to receive personal insight, as if the words adjust themselves to the seeker's own life. Third, Jesus spoke in parables to invite his listeners into contemplation. Rather than prescribing conclusions, parables create sacred space for reflection, where the soul becomes the interpreter.

PORTALS OF THE INNER KINGDOM: THREE PARABLES AS INVITATIONS TO THE MYSTICAL PATH

Jesus didn't lecture about enlightenment—he evoked it. His parables are not simply moral tales; they are spiritual devices, keys that unlock doors to deeper seeing. When held contemplatively, these stories do not just inform us—they transform us. Among the many he told, three stand out as potent portals —invitations to stages of the contemplative journey.

THE MUSTARD SEED: A PORTAL TO TRUST AND INNER GROWTH

> *"The kingdom of heaven is like a mustard seed..."*
> —Matthew 13:31-32

At first glance, this story appears quaint, even agricultural. But in the hands of a mystic, it becomes profound. Jesus invites us to see that the spiritual life often begins in obscurity—with something small, perhaps unnoticed by the world or ourselves. Yet, within that small beginning lies the expansive presence of God. The seed holds the tree. The hidden holds the holy.

The parable of the mustard seed reminds us that the Divine grows within us, silently, steadily, and always. Jesus' choice of the mustard seed—a tiny, seemingly insignificant seed that grows into a large plant—emphasizes the surprising and transformative power of the Kingdom of God. This growth, from humble beginnings to expansive presence, mirrors the inner spiritual journey, where faith, even as small as a mustard seed, can lead to profound transformation.

Moreover, the mustard plant's rapid and pervasive growth can be seen as a metaphor for the unstoppable spread of divine influence, both within the individual soul and throughout the world. This suggests that the Kingdom of God is not only a future hope but a present reality, growing and expanding in unexpected ways.

THE HIDDEN TREASURE AND THE PEARL: A PORTAL TO RECOGNITION AND DESIRE

> *"The kingdom of heaven is like treasure hidden in a field..."*
> —Matthew 13:44–46

In this brief parable, Jesus speaks of two seekers: one stumbles unexpectedly upon a hidden treasure; the other is actively searching and finally discovers a pearl of great price. Though their paths differ—one accidental, the other intentional—their response is the same. Each recognizes the overwhelming worth of what they've found and willingly gives up everything to obtain it.

This is the moment of spiritual awakening. Whether it arrives through a sudden moment of grace or after years of seeking, something within the soul recognizes a deeper truth—a glimpse of the divine, the sacred center, the kingdom within. It's not just an intellectual understanding, but a profound shift of the heart. The treasure or pearl represents the presence of God, the reality of divine love, or the soul's true home. And when we glimpse it, everything else loses its grip. Priorities reorder themselves. Attachments begin to fall away. We are drawn toward the treasure not by duty, but by desire—a longing to live in alignment with what we now know to be real.

These parables are portals to awakening. They speak to that moment when the veil thins, when the true self glimpses its divine nature. This is not mere intellectual assent; it is felt, known, and embodied. Once seen, it cannot be unseen. The treasure is worth every sacrifice. The pearl makes all else seem pale.

In this way, Jesus awakens our deep inner desire for union with the Beloved. The stories are not about greed or possession. They are about surrender—letting go of what is lesser to live for what is eternal.

THE PRODIGAL SON: A PORTAL TO RETURN AND UNION

> *"While he was still a long way off, his father saw him and was filled with compassion..."* —Luke 15:11–32

This story contains the entire mystical journey: departure, exile, suffering, awakening, and return. The son, lost in a foreign land, awakens to his longing and begins the walk home. What he finds is not judgment but embrace, not shame but celebration.

The Prodigal Son is a portal to grace. It reminds us that no matter how far we wander from our essence, our divine origin remains intact. The Parent in the story (symbolic of God) does not demand repentance first. He runs to the child, robes him in dignity, and restores him to wholeness.

This parable opens the contemplative heart to forgiveness, self-acceptance, and reunion with the Source. It teaches that the mystical path is not about earning love but remembering it was never lost.

LIVING THE PARABLES

These three parables do more than illustrate spiritual truths—they function as living metaphors for interior experience. They show us that:

- The journey begins with trusting the hidden (Mustard Seed),
- Awakens in a moment of recognition (Treasure and Pearl), and
- Finds wholeness in the return (Prodigal Son).

Held prayerfully, these stories become inner companions. They are not just Jesus' teachings; they are Jesus himself as teacher, gently leading us through the veils of illusion into the Kingdom that has always been within.

SILENCE, SOLITUDE, AND THE DESERT TRADITION

Jesus' mystical journey was marked by intentional retreats into solitude—times when he let go of the world to be fully present with God.. The Gospel of Mark (1:12-13) tells how, immediately after his baptism, the Spirit drove him into the wilderness, where he fasted and faced the temptations that sought to draw him back into ordinary perception.

This pattern—withdrawal, encounter, return—became a rhythm in Jesus' life. He taught the crowds with insight and power, then slipped away to pray, listen, and simply be. In these desert interludes, the "nothing" of the wilderness became his sanctuary. There, stripped of distractions, he discovered the living pulse of the Divine.

For Jesus, the desert was not merely empty land but a threshold of transformation. It was the place where illusions of identity, comfort, and control fell away, and reliance on God became absolute. In those silent expanses, he revealed the sacramental power of stillness, showing us that true revelation often arises when the mind grows quiet, words fall away, and the heart stands open before God.

Mysticism invites us into desert spaces—times of quiet, solitude, and reflection—where we can confront the voices that veil our true nature and awaken to the One who never leaves us.

THE HIDDEN APPRENTICESHIP: JOURNEYS BEYOND JUDEA

Between the boy who astonished the Temple teachers at twelve and the man who stepped from the Jordan's waters at thirty, there lies a silence in the Gospels—a span of years almost as veiled as the Temple's Holy of Holies. Mystics through the ages have called this Jesus' missing years or hidden apprenticeship, believing that during these years he traveled far beyond Galilee to train with the wisdom-keepers of the ancient world.

THE LOST YEARS AND THE LEGEND OF SAINT ISSA

The canonical Gospels provide scant details about Jesus' life between the ages of 12 and 30. This gap has given rise to various traditions and legends attempting to fill in the blanks. According to tradition, Jesus crossed into Egypt, studying sacred rites and healing arts with priestly lineages who guarded the mysteries of life and death. There, in the shadow of the pyramids, he is said to have learned how to blend compassion with medicine, reading the body's ailments as messages of the soul. This encapsulates the ancient Egyptian approach to healing, where medicine was deeply intertwined with spiritual understanding. In India, he is believed to have studied the Vedas under Brahmin priests in Puri and Rajgir, absorbing teachings on divine understanding and the laws of the great Buddha. His travels purportedly took him to the heights of the Himalayas, where yogis imparted the discipline of stillness and the power of inner light. In Tibet, he is said to have engaged with Buddhist monks, deepening his insights into compassion and selflessness. Further east, in China, Taoist masters are believed to have guided him in the art of *wu wei*—the principle of effortless action. This Taoist teaching emphasizes aligning one's actions with the natural flow of the universe, acting spontaneously and harmoniously without force or resistance. In embracing this philosophy, Jesus would have been absorbing the wisdom of living in harmony with the Tao, perceiving the unity that flows beneath every form, and cultivating a presence that responds to the world with grace and balance.

However, one of the most intriguing is the account of Saint Issa, as presented by Russian traveler Nicolas Notovitch in his 1894 publication, *The Unknown Life of Jesus Christ*. According to Notovitch, during a visit to the Hemis Monastery in Ladakh, India, he encountered ancient Tibetan scrolls detailing the life of a revered figure named Issa—a name closely resembling "Jesus" in Arabic. These texts describe Issa as a wise and compassionate teacher who traveled extensively through India, Nepal, and Tibet, studying and imparting spiritual wisdom. He is portrayed as someone who challenged social injustices, taught love and compassion, and sought to bridge the gaps between different faith traditions.

While the historical authenticity of Notovitch's claims has been debated, the narrative aligns with the idea of Jesus as a seeker of universal truths. It suggests that during his "lost years," Jesus may have engaged with diverse spiritual traditions, absorbing teachings that would later resonate in his own ministry.

This perspective invites us to consider that Jesus' teachings were not formed in isolation, nor confined to the boundaries of a single tradition. While the canonical Gospels remain silent on his formative years, enduring stories and cross-cultural legends suggest that Jesus may have journeyed beyond his homeland, perhaps eastward, engaging with wisdom traditions that spoke of unity, compassion, and the Divine within. Whether these stories are historically factual or symbolically rich, they point to a deeper spiritual reality: that true authority is not merely inherited, but awakened through prayerful seeking, encounter, and openness to the sacred in all its forms. In this light, Jesus' hidden years become not a gap, but an invitation to imagine a soul shaped by silence, mystery, and the universal longing to know God. It is a path that transcends institutions, echoing the truth that the Divine can be found wherever the heart listens.

As you reflect on his journeys, consider your own: Where might you go, within or beyond familiar shores, to learn the sacred arts of presence, compassion, and surrender? And like Jesus, how might you return to your community—not with a finished creed, but with a living message born of many voices, yet harmonized by one heart?

UNION CONSCIOUSNESS: "I IN YOU, YOU IN ME"

In the closing chapters of the Gospel of John, Jesus offers what is often called his high priestly prayer. But it is far more than a petition—it is a vision. In John 17, Jesus prays, "that they may all be one; just as you, Father, are in me, and I in you, that they also may be in us." This is not a metaphor, but a mystical reality. He is pointing toward the deepest truth of union consciousness—that the Divine dwells within us, and we dwell within the Divine.

For mystics, this prayer is not merely poetic. It is the heart of contemplative experience: the sense that the boundaries between self and the Divine source are permeable, even illusory. In this unity, separation dissolves. The drop knows it is part of the ocean. Julian of Norwich, the 14th-century English mystic, expressed this unity with God in her revelation: "God is nearer to us than our own soul." This isn't mere poetry—it's a mystical realization of shared being. In the contemplative heart, there is no distance between the seeker and the sought, the self and the Divine.

This is why the "I AM" sayings of Jesus carry profound mystical implications. When Jesus speaks in this way, he is not pointing to himself alone, but to the same Divine presence that spoke to Moses from the burning bush: "I AM that I AM." "I am the vine, you are the branches" (John 15:5) reveals an organic oneness, not hierarchy, but interconnected life. "I am the light of the world" (John 8:12) reminds us that light is not merely bestowed but shared and reflected. "I am the way, and the truth, and the life" (John 14:6) becomes, in the mystical reading, not a gatekeeping statement but a map of inner realization. The "I AM" speaks not only of Jesus, but of the Divine essence present in all.

Union consciousness invites us to awaken to the Divine essence we already share. It is not something to be attained, but something remembered. In prayer, meditation, or deep contemplation, we are not striving toward God—we are returning to the awareness from which we have never truly been separated

CONTEMPLATIVE PRAYER IN ACTION

The life of Jesus reveals prayer not merely as words spoken to God, but as a way of being with God. His most powerful moments of communion were often wordless, marked by presence, stillness, and surrender.

In the Garden of Gethsemane (Matthew 26:36–46), Jesus

enters a place of profound vulnerability. His prayer is not a polished petition, but a raw surrender: "Not my will, but Yours." This is the essence of contemplative prayer—trusting the will of the Divine even when the path ahead is dark. His stillness in the garden becomes a model for us: prayer as yielding, not because Jesus is passive, but because he's fully surrendered to Love's movement, even in fear or pain.

At the Transfiguration (Matthew 17:1–8), Jesus leads his closest companions up the mountain, where the veil briefly lifts, and divine radiance shines through him. No request is made. No teaching is given. Instead, they witness. This moment of pure being—of simply tasting the presence of the Divine—is at the heart of contemplative practice. Silence becomes revelation.

Again and again, Jesus models a posture not of asking or reminding God, but of listening. Whether in the wilderness, in solitude, or surrounded by crowds, he carries within him an unshakable attunement to the Father's presence. Contemplative prayer is not an escape from the world but a deeper entrance into it—with clarity, courage, and compassion born from inner stillness.

MIRACLES AS SYMBOLIC ACTS

The miracles of Jesus are not just wonders to be marveled at—they are signs. Each act points beyond itself, revealing the extraordinary hidden presence of God within the ordinary, the fearful, and the hungry. In every sign, there is a spiritual law at work: transformation, transcendence, abundance.

At Cana, water becomes wine—not through fanfare but presence. This is more than hospitality; it is the revelation that the mundane can become sacred. The ordinary becomes the extraordinary. Jesus doesn't conjure; he consecrates. The first sign in John's Gospel is not a display of power, but a whisper of divine joy woven into the fabric of daily life, where ordinary things become holy when offered and shared.

When he walks on water (Matthew 14:22–33), it is not to defy nature but to transcend fear. The storm rages, the waves rise, and the invitation comes: "Do not be afraid. It is I." Faith is not the absence of fear, but the willingness to step out, to trust the unseen ground beneath our feet. This miracle shows that union with the Divine allows us to move through life's turbulence with stillness at our center.

In the feeding of the five thousand (John 6:1-14), scarcity gives way to surplus. The miracle begins not with power but with gratitude. Jesus takes what little there is, gives thanks, and multiplies it in the act of blessing. This is the spiritual law of abundance: that what is given with love returns in fullness, pressed down and overflowing.

Each miracle is a portal—an unveiling. They teach not only what Jesus could do but also who we are invited to become: those who see the sacred in the simple, who walk through fear into trust, and who give from the heart will find there is always enough.

INCARNATION AND THE LIVING LOGOS

The Incarnation is not just a doctrine—it's a profound mystical reality: the eternal Word expressed through a human life, divine presence flowing through flesh and spirit. In Jesus, the invisible becomes visible—not because he is God incarnate, but because he embodied the divine Spirit so thoroughly that the sacred was manifest in human form. The infinite presence moved among the finite—not as a distant observer, but as one who chose to live fully within time, space, hunger, laughter, and tears..

John's Gospel opens with a profound mystery: "The Word became flesh and dwelt among us" (John 1:14). The Greek Logos

—the divine ordering principle, the sacred intelligence behind all creation—finds simple expression not in a palace but in a small, ordinary human life. In Jesus, the Logos—the living, divine Word—takes on flesh and moves, heals, touches, and listens in a uniquely tangible way.

But the mystical path doesn't end with Jesus. His Incarnation invites our own. If the Word can become flesh in him, then divine love can take form in each of us. Jesus is not only the bearer of divine presence—he is the pattern: "Christ in you." This is not a metaphor but a mystical reality calling us to become living tabernacles—imperfect yet present, surrendered rather than exalted. To follow Jesus as a mystic is to accept this invitation: to let the sacred express itself through our lives. We become vessels through which love speaks, heals, and serves—not in grand gestures, but in the quiet holiness of a kind act, a listening heart, a soul choosing presence.

EMBODYING THE MYSTICAL JESUS TODAY

To follow the Mystical Jesus is not to chase visions or escape this world. It is to root deeply into it—to let love become flesh once more, through our listening, our presence, and our practice. Jesus didn't just teach the Way; he was the Way. And his invitation remains: "Follow me."

In stillness, we learn to hear his voice—not as a sound, but as a deep inner knowing. In scripture and story, we meet him repeatedly—veiled in parables, radiant on mountaintops, kneeling in gardens. And in serving others, we find him in the faces, hands, and feet of those in need.

To embody Christ today is to live prayer with our lives, where a kind word becomes the mustard seed. A gesture of forgiveness becomes the return of the prodigal. A shared meal becomes the feeding of the five thousand. The mystical life isn't hidden in the clouds—it's hidden in plain sight, waiting to be lived.

Each day offers a choice: to pass by the sacred, or to pause and let it speak through us. To follow the Mystical Jesus is to see the Divine not just in him, but in ourselves and one another—until, at last, there are no more veils.

To walk the mystical path of Jesus is not to abandon spirituality—it is to reclaim it. But what does that path look like outside the walls of the Church? If faith isn't built around pews and pulpits, how do we still live it meaningfully?

In the next chapter, we'll examine real, grounded ways to nurture spirituality without religion—from meditation and contemplation to nature, dreams, and shared community.

AFFIRMATION

I open my heart to the Mystical Jesus.
I walk his path of silence, story, and service.
In me, the Kingdom is already here.

CHAPTER 4

SPIRITUALITY BEYOND THE CHURCH
PRACTICAL WAYS PEOPLE NURTURE FAITH OUTSIDE INSTITUTIONS

There is a longing in all of us—not necessarily for religion, but for connection. Connection to something greater than ourselves. We may use different words for it—God, Source, Spirit, the Divine—but the yearning is the same. It's the still, small voice we hear when the noise settles. It's the awe that takes our breath away beneath a starry sky. It's the tear we shed while listening to a beautiful piece of music or the sense of deep presence when holding the hand of someone we love.

For much of my life, the Church was where I found that connection. It gave me structure, language, and a sense of belonging. I served as a priest for over thirty years, baptizing infants, marrying lovers, and burying the dead. I prayed with the sick, sang the old hymns, and lifted the chalice high. There were moments of true holiness and moments of profound disillusionment.

Over time, I watched the Church change. Budgets began to matter more than blessings. Political alignments crept into sermons. Congregations shrank, but the business meetings grew. After my wife passed, the silence from the diocese was deafening. The place that once offered me spiritual refuge now felt hollow, as if the soul had slipped out while no one was looking.

And yet—I still believe.

I believe in a God who is present in all things, not just in sanctuaries. The Divine can be encountered in the rising of the sun, in the laughter of children, and in the deep exhale of meditation. I believe we do not need a priest to talk to God. We only need to listen, and we will hear Spirit speaking in our hearts, in our dreams, and in our very breath.

Stepping beyond the Church wasn't about abandoning God —it was stepping beyond the institution in search of deeper union with the Divine. That's an important distinction, because so many of us carry a quiet fear: that stepping away from Church means stepping away from God. But over time, often slowly and painfully, we begin to understand something more liberating: the Church may have held our faith, but it was never the source of it.

When I first moved beyond the Church, it felt like the ground had shifted beneath me. The familiar rhythms were gone. No weekly rituals. No hymns echoing into Monday morning. I missed the structure, the sacred pauses, the sense of being part of something larger than myself. But as the silence lengthened, something unexpected began to unfold. I started finding God in places I hadn't thought to look. The more profound truth emerged: stepping beyond the Church didn't take me further from God—it brought me closer.

In this season of my life, I've rediscovered practices that nourish my soul: prayer that feels like genuine conversation instead of performance; meditation that leads me inward to a sacred center; dreams carrying messages from a realm beyond reason; walks in nature where the Creator whispers through birdsong and wind; and moments of stillness where I hear God's voice—not from a pulpit, but within my own heart.

This is not a rejection of faith but a redirection—a conscious movement toward something more authentic. It's about finding the Divine in the rising sun, in grief and joy, and in quiet times of whispered prayers. It's learning to listen deeply and embrace a spirituality that grows from the stillness within rather than from external rituals alone.

This chapter does not reject the Church but recognizes that the Spirit moves beyond it. Jesus said, "Where two or three are gathered in my name, I am there." He never said it had to be in a cathedral.

WHAT MIGHT THIS SEARCH LOOK LIKE?

In my own journey, certain practices began to surface—gentle, grounding rituals that reminded me I wasn't alone. You may find yourself drawn to similar things:

- Interpreting what you've been shown in your dreams at the start of your day.
- Taking a slow walk at dusk, letting the colors of the sky speak their own language.
- Carrying a few sacred lines of scripture, poetry, or prose and holding them in your heart throughout the day.
- Lying awake at night, hand over heart, whispering, "Thank you."
- Listening for messages or noticing answers rising in still meditation.

These aren't rules. They're invitations—ways of remembering the sacred in the everyday. Many of these practices are described more fully in the appendix, should you wish to explore them further. This path is uniquely yours. No one else can walk it for you. And that, too, is part of its sacredness.

THE FEARS THAT ARISE

This journey is not without its emotional weight. Fear and guilt often travel with us when we leave the familiar. You may find yourself wondering:

- What if I'm doing it wrong?
- What if I drift too far from God?
- Without a community, will I be lazy and lose my spiritual rhythm?
- Can I grow without sermons and sacraments?

These are tender and honest questions. I've asked them too. But here's what I've come to trust: the same Spirit that stirred the hearts of prophets, mystics, and seekers lives within you. Your longing is not a flaw—it is sacred. The very act of questioning reveals your hunger for something real, something lasting. Even your doubt is a kind of prayer.

You are not lost. You are being led. You are not lazy. You are awakening.

And while you may no longer sit in a pew or recite a creed, you are already standing in sacred space—because God has never needed a building to find you. All he has ever needed is... you.

REASSURANCE FOR THE JOURNEY

You are not alone. Quietly, worldwide, people are stepping away from institutional religion—not out of apathy or because their faith is fading—but because they yearn for something more genuine. They gather—not to debate doctrine, but to share stories about love, loss, healing, and Spirit.

Spirituality beyond the Church often demands more honesty, courage, and trust. It invites you to become a mystic in your own right—to know God not secondhand but through your own breath and being. It requires us to take responsibility for our own relationship with God, to seek, to question, and to listen. It invites us to become people who know God not through dogma but through direct experience.

Spirituality beyond the Church doesn't mean walking without support. Support is still there. It just looks different. It may be a friend who listens without judging. A poem that opens your soul. A dog who watches the sunrise beside you. A bird that returns each day to your windowsill.

So we can begin here, with openness and a willingness to see the sacred in new ways. Let us remember: as Scripture says, the veil of the temple was torn, signifying God's presence now everywhere.

And the Church, though faltering, was never meant to be the only path to God. Our hearts were. The path ahead may be quieter. It may lack the structure you're used to. But it will be alive. So is God. And so are you.

As we begin to form a more personal and experiential faith, old voices may rise up—voices of guilt, shame, or unworthiness. Religion taught many of us that we must earn God's love, follow rules, or be "good enough."

But true spirituality calls us to release that burden. The next chapter is about letting go—so we can remember who we really are and how deeply we are already loved.

AFFIRMATION

Sacred One,
You are not far off, but near.

Not confined to temples, but alive in trees, breath, and silence.
Help me release fear.
Could you help me trust my steps?
Let me find you in the quiet and carry you in the ordinary.
May my heart be the altar,
My breath be the hymn,
My life be the sanctuary.

CHAPTER 5
RELEASING GUILT
RETURNING TO THE SACRED PATH
OF YOUR OWN SOUL

For many, the idea of seeking God beyond the Church stirs a quiet, often unspoken guilt. From childhood, we're taught that true faith must be anchored in church attendance, sacraments, and doctrine. To explore God elsewhere—in nature, silence, dreams, or deep stillness—can feel like a betrayal of the very faith that once formed us.

But this guilt doesn't come from Jesus. It comes from structures built around Him. Jesus did not come to create an institution or prescribe rigid rituals. He came to awaken hearts and restore a direct, unmediated relationship with the Divine. His earliest followers weren't called Christians. They were called People of the Way—men and women walking a path of love, transformation, and daily communion with God.

Faith, as Jesus taught it, is a matter of the heart. He called us to compassion, forgiveness, justice, and awakening—qualities that transcend any building or belief system. The early followers of Jesus lived their faith in streets, homes, and wilderness paths—not through ceremony, but through awareness, simplicity, and communion with the Living Light.

And that Light, the Christ-consciousness, still flickers

within us, quietly urging us inward, not toward dogma, but toward direct encounter.

THE ROOTS OF GUILT

So, where does this guilt come from?

It runs deep. Many of us were conditioned to believe that seeking God outside the Church is misguided—even dangerous. We were taught that stepping away from ritual was the same as stepping away from God. And so we carry a quiet fear: that our spiritual hunger might lead us astray.

But the Gospel tells a different story—one of inner awakening and Divine indwelling.

Historically, much of this guilt stems from how the institutional Church evolved. After Constantine's reign and the Council of Nicaea, the Church began to shape a system grounded in uniformity, hierarchy, and external control. Over time, this structure often replaced the intimate, mystical experience of God that Jesus both embodied and encouraged.

Jesus frequently challenged the religious authorities of his time. He pointed not to rigid systems, but to an inward path marked by humility, sincerity, and love. He reminded us that the sacred isn't confined to temples—but lives within the hearts of those who seek truth and stillness.

The earliest followers understood this. Their faith wasn't bound to buildings, but rooted in the living presence of the Holy in all things. They gathered in homes and open fields, shared dreams and visions, and listened for the still, small voice that spoke not through hierarchy, but through the soul.

So why should we feel bound to structures Jesus never imposed?

God is not confined to pews, pulpits, or stained glass. The Divine meets us in stillness, kindness, creation, and the quiet longing of our souls. The sacred lives as much in the forest as in the sanctuary. Jesus called it the Kingdom within—a truth awakened not by formality, but by presence, love, and the courage to listen inward.

LETTING GO OF GUILT

To release guilt is to untangle yourself from illusion. It begins by naming guilt for what it is: not divine truth, but inherited tradition. Our connection to the Divine isn't something we earn through compliance—it's something we awaken to through love.

The belief that we must go through the Church to reach God is a human construct, not a commandment. The early Jesus movement thrived without hierarchy or buildings. It was a living faith expressed in love, courage, healing, and radical inclusion.

When you seek God in silence, solitude, or beneath an open sky, you're listening to the sacred whisper that lives within your soul. That pursuit is no less holy than prayers said in a pew or hymns sung in a cathedral.

Here is the liberating truth: the Church does not have exclusive access to God. It may offer community and guidance, but it cannot contain the Divine.

God is present in every sunrise, every loving gesture, every shared tear. God is in the breath, in the dream that wakes you at midnight, in the unspoken knowing that comes when you sit beneath stars and feel your soul stirred.

Seeking the sacred in these moments is not a departure from faith—it is its fulfillment.

PRACTICES FOR RELEASING GUILT AND SEEKING GOD

Affirm Your Inherent Worth
You are inherently worthy of a relationship with God. The Divine lives in you, moves through you, and yearns to be known with you. That connection is sacred, wherever it unfolds.

See the Sacred in All Things
Open your heart to the presence of God in the hush of early morning, in the wind rustling through trees, or in the soul of a stranger. The veil is thin—if only we have eyes to see.

Let Go of Limiting Beliefs
The teachings of your past may have shaped your journey, but they need not restrict it. Let go of the idea that God is found only in specific places or forms.

Make Room for the Divine
Carve out quiet moments—for prayer, meditation, contemplation, or a slow walk under moonlight. These are doorways to the Holy.

Walk Your Own Sacred Path
You do not need permission to seek God in the way your soul is called. Trust your inner compass. Honor your unfolding path. The Spirit speaks in the language you best understand.

A LIVING FAITH

Remember, letting go of the guilt that comes from seeking God beyond the Church is not a rejection of faith—it is a return to its essence. Your relationship with the Divine is sacred and deeply personal—no institution can define it, nor tradition can contain it. As you release that inherited guilt, you may discover a deeper, more authentic connection with God—one not rooted in obligation, but in love. Faith becomes not a static system, but a living expression of your soul's longing and the Divine's response.

Jesus never said the path to God would be uniform. He said it was narrow, not because it excludes, but because it is uniquely personal. Each journey to the Divine is shaped by wonder, surrender, and the courage to listen.

Letting go of guilt is not a loss—it is a liberation. It is not a departure from faith but a return to its beating heart. Along that path, you may find what was true all along: That the God you seek has never been confined by walls but has always walked beside you, even when you stepped beyond the Church doors. Even when you didn't yet know how deeply you were already held.

Once guilt begins to fall away, something beautiful emerges: longing. A hunger not for structure but for communion, not for answers but for presence. That yearning is not emptiness—it's the soul awakening.

In the next chapter, we'll follow that longing into what it truly is: a call to something more. A sacred invitation that has always been within you.

AFFIRMATION

I am worthy of divine connection.
I release all guilt inherited from human systems.
The sacred lives within me, around me,
and calls to me in the quiet.

*My journey is holy. My seeking is blessed.
I walk freely with the Presence
who has always walked with me.*

CHAPTER 6
A CALL TO SOMETHING MORE

There comes a moment in life when the familiar no longer satisfies. It's not necessarily a crisis of faith or a rejection of what once brought comfort, but rather a quiet whisper in the soul that says, There is more.

For years, I walked the well-worn path of tradition, finding solace in the Church's rituals, prayers, and the rhythm of community life. It had beauty—a sense of belonging and a connection to something ancient and enduring. And yet, beneath it all, a deeper hunger lingered. A yearning stirred for something more intimate, something that couldn't be contained within walls or creeds—a desire for union, not merely understanding.

At first, I mistook this restlessness for a need to do more—more reading, more service, more study. But no matter how much I immersed myself in the Church's teachings, the longing remained. It wasn't about doctrine or duty. It was about relationship. I didn't want to merely know about God—I wanted to know God. Not through intermediaries or inherited beliefs, but through direct, unmediated experience.

This chapter is about that yearning—a journey from faith

as an institution to faith as lived mysticism. It marks a shift from belief shaped by external authority to a communion nurtured from within. Even when the Church seemed to turn away, I discovered that God never had. The Divine was never confined to sacred buildings but had always dwelled in the quiet corners of the heart, in the stillness of contemplation, and in the extraordinary moments of everyday life.

The call to seek God beyond the Church is not a rejection of the past but an invitation to go deeper. It is a turning inward—a willingness to trust that the Divine speaks not only through scripture or clergy, but also through the quiet language of our own souls, dreams, and daily awakenings.

And so, the search began.

There's a profound difference between believing in God because you've been taught to, and coming to know God through direct experience. It's like reading about the ocean versus standing at its edge, feeling the tide pull at your feet. For years, I stood on the shore, content with the descriptions, reassured by the voices telling me what the water was like. But something in me longed to wade in—to feel the depths for myself.

It was in stillness, outside of sermons and rituals, that I began to sense God differently. In quiet contemplation, early morning prayer, and the gentle knowing that sometimes comes in dreams, I encountered something deeper than doctrine could hold. These were not grand revelations but quiet, personal encounters: a presence in the rustling of leaves, the flicker of candlelight, the deep peace that sometimes arises even in sorrow—the veil between the seen and unseen thinned.

The realization came slowly, like the dawn breaking: God was already here, always speaking, always present. The sacred was everywhere—in nature, in silence, and in the seemingly ordinary moments of life that, upon closer reflection, revealed themselves as anything but ordinary.

This journey from institutional to experiential faith wasn't about abandoning the past but about opening up to something more profound. It wasn't about discarding what once guided me, but recognizing that the truest authority—-the most authentic connection to God—must be cultivated within. It marked a shift from seeking validation outside to seeking truth within; from hearing about God to tasting the Divine Presence for myself.

And so, I began to trust that inner voice. Prayer became less a formula and more a living conversation. Meditation became my sanctuary—a place where God spoke in silence. Each day became a dialogue with the Divine, where lessons unfolded through grief, joy, and the miracle of simply being alive.

Faith was no longer about watching from the shore. It was about stepping into the water, feeling the current, and trusting I would not sink.

GLIMPSES ALONG THE WAY

These mystical glimpses were sacred thresholds—thin places where Spirit whispered louder than words.

1. *A Moment in Nature*

One night, I sat alone beneath a vast expanse of sky, far from the noise and weight of daily life. The air was still, save for the occasional whisper of wind through the trees. Above me, the heavens stretched endlessly. I viewed a sea of stars shimmering like distant embers, all the while amazed to know their light had traveled eons to meet my eyes.

For a long while, I simply watched. I had always known the stars were there, but how often had I truly seen them? In the busyness of life, they'd become little more than faint sparkles of light dimmed by artificial glow and mental clutter. But here, in the silence, they came alive—burning, breathing, speaking in a language older than time.

Something stirred within me—a feeling beyond words. It wasn't the structured, predictable faith of Sunday mornings. There was no sermon, no scripture—only presence. A deep knowing that I was part of something infinitely greater, yet intimately held within it.

Then I understood what the Psalmist meant: "Be still, and know that I am God."

God wasn't distant—not confined to sanctuaries or rituals. God was here, in the quiet hum of the universe, in the rhythm of my breath, in the stillness within. I had come looking for nothing in particular—and somehow, I found everything.

2. A Dream That Spoke Louder Than a Sermon

Dreams have always intrigued me. Even as a child, I sensed they were more than fragments of thought—perhaps messages from a realm beyond. Science might reduce them to neural noise, but I've experienced otherwise. I've received visions, insights, and glimpses of the beyond in dreams.

After Charlene passed, when grief was raw and unrelenting, I longed for something beyond reason. Then one night, a dream came—so vivid, so real—it renewed everything I believed.

I stood in a space bathed in golden light. No landscape, no sky—just a vast presence of peace. And there was Charlene.

Radiant. Untouched by pain or sorrow. Not as I had last seen her, but as I had always known her—whole and luminous. Her eyes, deep and knowing, met mine with a love so complete it filled every empty space within me.

She spoke gently, "Honey, I am always right beside you. I am always with you."

Peace flooded through me. I knew then—without doubt—

that she was alive. Not bound by time or form, but alive in a way more real than words can express.

No sermon, no theology, no book had ever given me that certainty. It was a message beyond doctrine. The Divine had spoken—in the personal, silent language of the soul.

3. A Mother's Day Message: Love Through Synchronicity

This past Mother's Day was especially difficult. The ache of missing Charlene felt heavy, but the day unfolded with moments that felt anything but random—like she was reaching out, gently reminding me she's still near.

It began when I went down to the cellar to grab the blower so I could clear the deck of pollen. As I moved past some old belongings, I noticed Charlene's sewing chair tucked in the corner. Something nudged me to open the storage compartment beneath the seat, a place she used to keep odds and ends. Inside, folded neatly, was a piece of paper. I opened it and found a handmade Mother's Day card from our children—an old one, full of crayon love and childhood joy. I stood there holding it, and the tears came. It felt as if Charlene had left it there for me to find, just when I needed it most.

Later, still carrying the weight of the day, I decided to take a drive and clear my head. As I backed out of the driveway, the radio was playing an old episode of Casey Kasem's Top 40, a show from the 1990s. As I pulled away, I heard a young woman dedicate a song to her parents for their anniversary. She spoke about how, when they were first married, they had nothing— but they had each other, and their love carried them through.

It was our story. May 1st had just marked what would have been our 44th anniversary. Charlene and I started with nothing —we even charged our wedding on a Mastercard—but we built a beautiful life together, rich in love and meaning.

Then came the song she had requested: Through the Years

by Kenny Rogers. That was our song. I had said those very words to Charlene not long before she passed: "Honey, we had the best life." And she smiled and replied, "Just like Kenny Rogers' Through the Years."

I cried again—but this time because I knew, without a doubt, she was with me. Speaking to me. Reminding me of the love we shared—and that it still lives on.

What began as a day of grief became a tender, soul-stirring reminder of connection. That wasn't just a coincidence—it was communion. Synchronicity. Charlene reached through the veil with signs so intimately woven into our shared life that only I would recognize them: her sewing chair, a forgotten Mother's Day card, a radio broadcast from decades past playing our song and telling our story. Each thread of the day was stitched with love and intention.

Grief opens a space where the sacred can slip in—if we're willing to feel. And I did. I wept, remembering and receiving. These are the moments I've written about so often: the extraordinary hidden in the ordinary. They affirm that love, real love, never dies. It just changes form. Charlene is still showing up, still celebrating anniversaries, and still listening to our hearts.

4. The Silence That Spoke Volumes

For much of my life, prayer had been structured—words, intercessions, traditions. I led congregations, offered prayers of comfort, and taught others how to pray. Yet often, I filled the silence with words, unsure if I was truly listening.

After Charlene's passing, that changed. Grief stripped everything down. Familiar words felt hollow.

But in the stillness of meditation, something else emerged.

There, in silence, I felt her—not a memory, not wishful

thinking, but a presence. Whole. Radiant. Not gone, but here, now.

In that sacred silence, I understood: God hadn't abandoned me. God had simply shifted the language.

I no longer prayed for answers. I listened. I rested. I communed. And in that communion, I no longer needed proof—because love, presence, and peace were enough.

5. *The Unexpected Kindness of a Stranger*

One of the most sacred moments I've experienced didn't happen in a church. It happened in a quiet café at the local senior center.

It had been a hard day. Grief sat heavy in my chest like a silent companion. I sat alone, sipping coffee, searching for comfort in routine. That's when a stranger nearby caught my eye.

He approached gently and asked if he could sit. I nodded. He didn't try to fix anything or fill the silence with platitudes. He simply sat, present, kind, and real.

We spoke a little, but it was enough. In that moment, I felt seen, not as a pastor or a grieving husband, but as a soul.

He didn't preach. He didn't quote scripture. But in that quiet act of human kindness, he became the hands and heart of Christ.

IN SUMMARY

This chapter explored the sacred transition from a faith rooted in institutional tradition to one grounded in personal experience and mystical knowing. It spoke to the deep yearning many feel—not for more doctrine, but for more profound communion. Through moments of silence, dreams, nature, and human kindness, I've come to see that God is not confined to church walls, but is found in the inner sanctuary of the soul.

The Divine calls us to something more—not to discard our past, but to carry forward what is living and true. Once we recognize that the Sacred speaks beyond pews and pulpits, a more personal question arises: How do I now live in response to this Presence?

That question leads us to practice, not rules, but rhythms. Not dogma, but devotion. If Part One named the ache, Part Two begins to answer it—not with rigid formulas, but with living, breathing invitations to encounter the Divine. In this next section, we'll explore how prayer, dreams, silence, and everyday moments become new altars—ways we meet God beyond the Church, yet still in sacred rhythm.

AFFIRMATION

I will trust the still, sacred voice within me.
God is not distant, but intimately near
—in silence, dreams, and every breath I take

PART TWO
PRACTICES FOR A LIVING FAITH

"Do not look for the Kingdom of God here or there. The Kingdom of God is within you." —Luke 17:21

The journey of spiritual awakening does not end with longing —it begins there. When we finally recognize that our yearning for the Divine cannot be satisfied by institutions alone, a new path opens. This path is inward, intimate, alive, and with each other. It does not require formal permission or sacred credentials, only willing hearts and listening souls.

In this part of the book, we explore the sacred tools that help awaken and deepen our relationship with each other and the Divine, not through rigid obligation but through daily attentiveness. These practices are not reserved for monks or mystics; they are available for all who are seekers. They are how we live out our connection with God in our homes, our grief, our joy, and the ordinary rhythms of life.

You won't find rigid rules here. Instead, you'll find invitations. Invitations to listen deeply. To pray without pretense. To discover that your dreams might be divine messages. That silence may be your holiest sanctuary. That God's presence is not rare, but constant, waiting to be noticed in each breath and step.

This is also the territory of the mystic: not a person removed from the world, but one fully immersed in it, attuned to the sacred pulsing beneath the surface of all things. As you step into these pages, I invite you to bring only one thing: your willingness to open your heart to the possibility that God has always been speaking—you simply needed new ways to listen.

CHAPTER 7
HOW DO I FIND GOD BEYOND THE CHURCH?

For many of us, the Church once offered a spiritual home—a place where God could be found through ritual, community, and sacred space. But what happens when the institution no longer speaks to the soul—when prayers feel hollow, sermons sound political, and God seems strangely absent from the pews?

This chapter offers a starting point—a few practices that have helped me reconnect with the Divine beyond the traditional framework. These aren't complex or exotic. They're simple, intentional ways to open our lives to the sacred—practices like meditation, contemplation, time in nature, and listening to the wisdom that arises from within. And while we'll go deeper into some of these in later chapters, what matters most is the spirit in which they're done: not as tasks to perform, but as invitations into God's presence.

So, where do we begin? For me, the journey didn't begin with disillusionment—it began long before, in years of prayer, meditation, and ministry. But something shifted after decades in the Church, when the pews grew quieter and the sermons no longer stirred my soul the way a calm morning walk often did.

The sacred began to show up not only in liturgy but also in stillness, not only in church music but also in breath and birdsong.

If I were to begin the search for God beyond the Church, I would begin with presence. Learning to recognize the divine in the ordinary. Here's how I'd approach it:

1. SILENCE AND STILLNESS: THE FIRST TEMPLE

God often whispers. To hear that whisper, we must quiet the noise. I'd start by creating space for silence, free from distractions, through meditation or contemplative prayer. This isn't about mastering a technique—it's about being present. I've found that when the mind slows, when breath becomes intentional, the soul begins to speak. After Charlene passed, I struggled for weeks to find that stillness again. But one day, in meditation, everything flowed. In that silence, she was there. God was there. The veil had thinned—because I had become still enough to notice.

Even five minutes a day can open the door to the divine. In silence, we don't need to speak—we need only to listen.

2. NATURE AS A CATHEDRAL

I've felt God in chapels—but more vividly, I've found the divine while walking in nature, by the ocean, and beneath the night sky. The Creator's presence often feels more immediate outdoors, where no liturgy is required. When I walked with Cooper, my beloved dog, there were moments when the wind through the trees felt like the breath of God. The earth pulses with sacred energy—if we're willing to slow down and feel it.

Nature isn't just a backdrop for spirituality. It is a sanctuary —a living cathedral where every bird, breeze, and sunrise offers a silent message.

3. THE LANGUAGE OF DREAMS AND INTUITION

Dreams have long been a sacred channel for divine communication. Some of my most profound spiritual insights didn't come from books or sermons but through the quiet hours of the night. These dreams felt like more than imagination—they were vivid, meaningful, and carried a sacred presence that lingered long after waking. They offered clarity, reassurance, and a sense of being deeply held by something greater than myself.

Start by keeping a dream journal. Ask for guidance as you drift into sleep, and over time, patterns and messages may begin to emerge. Intuition works in much the same way—a quiet nudge, a deep knowing, or an unexpected peace after a choice is made. These moments, subtle yet powerful, often mark the nearness of the Divine.

4. ACTS OF LOVE AND KINDNESS

Where there is love, there is God. You don't need a pulpit to preach this gospel. Every act of compassion—every moment we choose kindness over convenience—is a spiritual practice. In my own season of loss, I found God in the gentle check-ins from friends, the warm smile of a stranger, and the quiet presence of someone who simply sat with me.

We reflect God not by professing belief but by practicing love. The divine flows through our hands when we serve, listen, and uplift.

5. LEARNING FROM MYSTICS AND WISDOM TRADITIONS

Some of my richest spiritual nourishment has come from the mystics—Meister Eckhart, Julian of Norwich, St. John of the

Cross—and from teachers beyond my tradition. Edgar Cayce, often called the "sleeping prophet," and the channeled teachings of The Law of One also speak of the soul's journey, divine unity, and the power of inner knowing. Like the Christian mystics, they remind us that God is not confined to institutions, but meets us in direct experience, deep silence, and sacred solitude.

I want to encourage you to explore this topic more widely. Read the Bhagavad Gita, listen to Paramahamsa Yogananda, engage the writings of Edgar Cayce or the Law of One, and let truth echo where it may. God is not threatened by curiosity.

6. SEEKING SIGNS AND SYNCHRONICITIES

Pay attention to the small things—a song on the radio that speaks to your heart, a feather on the path, an old friend who calls at the exact right moment. These are not mere coincidences—they are divine winks, reminders that we are seen, known, and loved.

Once you begin to notice them, you'll see them everywhere. These signs are breadcrumbs on the path home.

7. CREATING A NEW SACRED SPACE

You don't need stained glass to feel awe. Create space for spiritual community wherever you are. I've found depth in casual gatherings—over coffee, or during Theology on Tap nights where people meet in a pub and talk honestly about God, doubt, and life.

Your sacred circle might meet in a living room or a garden. What matters is presence, openness, and a shared hunger for the sacred. A spiritual life beyond the Church is not solitary—it's communal, but on different terms.

To seek God beyond the Church is not to leave the sacred

behind—it is to discover it anew: alive, uncontained, and ever near. The Divine is not confined to liturgy or doctrine, but moves through the rustle of trees, the silence of meditation, the kindness of strangers, and the wisdom of dreams.

If you're asking the question, then you've already begun the journey.

Welcome.

As we find God beyond the Church—in silence, in nature, in acts of love, and in the simple rhythms of life—we begin to realize something profound: the sacred is not only all around us—it is speaking to us. The Divine rarely shouts. It whispers through intuition, dreams, and moments of stillness that draw us inward.

To sense these subtle movements of Spirit, we must learn to slow down and truly listen.

In the next chapter, we'll explore this deeper posture of attentiveness, because before we can follow God's voice, we must first learn how to hear it.

AFFIRMATION

I am never alone on this path.
Each breath draws me closer to the Divine,
and each moment of love connects me to the greater whole.
I walk with presence, and I walk with others
—even if I have not yet met them.

CHAPTER 8
THE LISTENING LIFE
DREAMS, MEDITATION, AND THE LANGUAGE OF SPIRIT

WHISPERS FROM THE SOUL

In the previous chapter, I touched on practices like meditation, contemplation, time in nature, and attentive presence as ways to find God beyond the Church. But here, I want to go deeper—not just into the how, but into the why. Because underneath all spiritual seeking lies a fundamental truth: to know God, we must learn to listen.

This kind of listening isn't something the Church often taught us to cultivate. It favored outward rituals over inner silence, structured prayers over the simple language of the soul. But in my experience, it's in the stillness—beneath the surface of everyday life—that Divine guidance begins to emerge.

For me, this journey became more intense after Charlene passed. I found myself unmoored—not just emotionally, but spiritually. The rituals I had once clung to felt hollow. The words of the liturgy no longer reached the tender places of my heart. But in the long nights and quiet mornings, something new took root—an inner knowing that God was not absent. God was waiting. Waiting in the silence, the ache, the space where words had run out, I began to listen. Not outwardly, but inwardly, in meditation, dreams, and moments of quiet contemplation.

These practices became a lifeline, pulling me from despair into a place of stillness and clarity. They became doorways into divine dialogue. Because when we learn to listen from within, the soul begins to hear God everywhere.

DREAMS: SACRED MESSENGERS AND THE LANGUAGE OF THE SOUL

Dreams are not random firings of the brain—they are scripture written by the soul. Many traditions have honored dreams as channels of divine communication. The Bible contains them: Joseph's guidance to flee with Mary and Jesus came in a dream. Jacob wrestled with God by night. Daniel interpreted royal dreams as visions from heaven.

In my own life, I've had dreams that brought comfort, guidance, and even gentle warnings. Some were simple; others lingered, leaving me pondering their meaning for days. One dream in particular—shortly before my dog Cooper passed—showed me the ache of goodbye before it came. I saw him walking away into the distance, peaceful but unreachable. I didn't fully understand it until later, but it prepared my spirit in ways I couldn't have anticipated

I keep a dream journal by my bed to honor these sacred messages. Upon waking, I write whatever fragments I remember, even a single image. Then I sit with that image in contemplation and ask: What truth am I being shown beneath the surface? Over time, patterns emerge. And through those patterns, wisdom unfolds.

We don't need to decode dreams like puzzles. Instead, we ask: What part of me is speaking? What is my soul trying to show me? A snake might mean transformation. A locked door could be an invitation to knock.

Symbols don't explain—they reveal. Jesus himself taught through symbolic language: "I am the vine," "I am the bread of life," "I am the door." These metaphors carry layers of truth, waiting to unfold within us.

When a symbol appears—perhaps in a dream or daily life—ask: What does this mean to me personally? Let the symbol become your teacher. Return to it in prayer. Let it evolve over time.

MEDITATION: CREATING SPACE FOR PRESENCE

If dreams come in sleep, meditation is our way of dreaming awake. It's where we clear space in the mind—not to think, but to be, to listen without fixing, to wait without grasping.

I often begin by sitting in silence—just me, my breath, and the quiet invitation to be still. But there are days when the noise in my mind is loud, when grief or distraction refuses to settle. In those moments, I turn to tools like guided audio meditations. They don't do the work for me, but they create a gentle rhythm that helps still the mental waters and open the heart.

Whether sitting quietly, walking through nature, or simply breathing deeply, the essence of meditation is sacred attention. Some days, there is only quiet. No voice. No vision. But even in the silence, something sacred rests. And sometimes, amid that quiet, clarity arises—subtle but sure. A nudge. A word. A knowing.

CONTEMPLATION: LETTING THE HEART SPEAK

Contemplation, to me, is the soul's way of chewing on truth. It's not analysis—it's reverence. It's when we sit with a dream, a line of Scripture, or a stirring in our hearts and ask: What is this teaching me? What is God saying here?

This isn't a fast process. It's slow and patient—like steeping tea. I often find that insights don't come in the moment of sitting, but hours or days later. A spontaneous connection forms. A truth clicks into place.

Sometimes, when I'm uncertain whether a message is truly from God or simply from my own mind, I ask:

- Does this message bring peace?
- Does it honor love?
- Does it align with my deepest sense of truth?

The Spirit never shames. Never frightens. Never rushes. Never demands.

Divine guidance may challenge us, but it always leads toward compassion and wholeness.

SYNCHRONICITY: THE UNIVERSE AS MIRROR

Carl Jung spoke of synchronicity as a meaningful coincidence —events so perfectly timed they seem orchestrated by something greater. When the same phrase appears in a book, a dream, and a stranger's words in the same week, we are wise to pause. These are not mere coincidences. They are patterns rising from the deep—moments when the outer world aligns with the inner soul. Some call this the guidance of Spirit, while others see it as the whisper of God.

Reflect at day's end:

What unexpected alignments or symbols showed up today? What felt like a wink from the universe? Keep a synchronicity journal to track recurring themes.

LEARNING TO TRUST THE INNER VOICE

For many of us raised in the Church, trusting our inner voice can feel dangerous. We were taught to defer to authority and to distrust the self. But if we are, as Scripture says, made in the image of God—if the Spirit truly dwells within—then it follows that Divine wisdom can rise up from within as well. What once seemed like rebellion—listening within instead of outwardly—has become the most faithful act of trust for me.

That doesn't mean we won't get it wrong sometimes. But that's okay. Listening is a practice, not a perfection. And in my experience, when I pause, ask, and truly listen, God is never far.

The inner life—the listening life—is not a replacement for community, but it is the foundation of spiritual authenticity. Without it, religion becomes performance. With it, even the most ordinary moment becomes a meeting place with the Divine.

A LIFE LIVED FROM THE INSIDE OUT

I've come to believe that we don't need a pulpit to hear God. We need a quiet corner, a journal, a walk beneath the trees, and a willingness to be still. This is the listening life. It's less about answers and more about presence. Less about certainty and more about openness. And ultimately, it's about learning to trust that the Divine who made you also speaks within you.

So pause. Listen. The Sacred is speaking—maybe not in thunder or scripture—but in dream, in breath, in stillness. And that voice? It's meant for you—gentle, wise, and quietly insistent. All it asks is that you make room to hear it— and trust that the whisper is Love calling you home.

As we learn to listen—to our dreams, to silence, to the still, small voice of the Spirit—we begin to sense something deeper: a longing not only for divine connection, but for human relationships that reflect the same sacred qualities—depth, love, and attentiveness—we've come to cherish in our walk with the Divine. The journey inward often awakens a yearning outward—for kindred spirits, for heart-centered conversations, for companions who honor mystery and speak the language of the soul. Solitude teaches us to hear, but it is in relationship that we are called to live what we've heard.

The spiritual path, while personal, was never meant to be solitary. Others are listening, too. And when we meet them, something sacred unfolds. In the next chapter, we'll explore what it means to find—and be—a companion on the journey. Because somewhere out there, others are listening too.

AFFIRMATION

I open my heart to the gentle voice within.
In silence, in dreams, and in sacred pause,
I hear the soul speak. I am not alone.
I am deeply guided, wholly held, and forever
connected to the Divine whisper within.

CHAPTER 9

A SPIRITUALITY OF COMPANIONSHIP

Many of us carry a quiet ache—a longing not just for God, but for companions who truly see and understand us. As our relationship with the Divine deepens, so too does our desire for human connection that reflects that same sacred depth. We yearn for others who listen inwardly, who walk gently with mystery, who speak in the language of the soul.

This longing for connection often intensifies after leaving the institutional Church. People walk away for many reasons—spiritual dryness, disillusionment, or the sense that the Church has traded mystery for politics and control. Yet even as we step away from its walls, a deeper hunger remains: the desire for authentic spiritual community. We miss what the Church, at its best, once offered—a circle of seekers, a shared rhythm of worship, purpose, and wonder. We don't stop longing for belonging—we just start looking for it in new, more meaningful ways.

That's where a new kind of spirituality takes root—a spirituality that thrives in the bonds we form with those who walk beside us. It's not built on shared doctrines, but on shared journeys. Each of us is on a path to know the Divine, but it is in the company of others—those who ask the hard questions, offer their hearts, and dare to be vulnerable—that we discover the deepest richness.

THE DEEP LONGING FOR COMPANIONSHIP

I've noticed that many people who step away from the Church don't just grieve the loss of ritual—they grieve the loss of companionship. Church wasn't only a place of prayer or doctrine. It was where we gathered in a shared search for God. We listened, questioned, and supported one another in ways that formed a kind of family—a family that transcended bloodlines and, for many, felt more meaningful than any other.

But what happens when that family is no longer there? Where do we find connection, companionship, and support as we continue our search for God—this time in a way that honors our individuality and freedom of spirit?

I've come to believe that the human need for companionship—for kindred souls—is not something we outgrow on the spiritual path. It's part of the path itself. That's why Spirituality on Tap has taken off so beautifully. It's not a church, but a circle of seekers. It's about connection, not conformity. It's about sharing our stories, doubts, dreams, and encounters with the Divine—with people who don't have to agree with us, but who are willing to walk with us.

THE POWER OF SHARED JOURNEY

When we find a group of people who are also on a spiritual path, whether they are religious, agnostic, or just curious, something powerful happens. We stop feeling like we're isolated in our journey. We begin to see that others are struggling, questioning, and searching just like we are. And in that shared search, God speaks. Not in the grand sermons or theological debates, but in the quiet understanding that passes between us when we are truly seen and heard by another soul.

That's why companionship is so sacred. It's not about being in a room of people who all believe the same thing. It's about being with people who are brave enough to share their doubts and experiences. People who are open to the mysteries of life, who ask the hard questions, and who are willing to search together for answers. It's about creating a space where you can be yourself—without judgment—and where your spiritual growth is nurtured by the support of others.

CREATING A COMMUNITY OF SEEKERS

So how do we create these circles of spiritual companionship? We begin by recognizing that we don't need a church building to host a sacred gathering, an ordained minister to lead it, or a formal structure to make it real. All we need are open hearts—and a willingness to see the Divine in one another.

It might start with a few friends gathered around a table, sharing a meal and talking about life, faith, and the things that stir their hearts. Maybe it's a quiet conversation over coffee with someone who dares to ask about your spiritual journey. Or perhaps it's a small group coming together to meditate, reflect on dreams, or explore the teachings of different traditions, without pressure to conform to any single path.

Wherever they begin, these gatherings don't need to be formal or polished. They don't need an agenda. What they need is intention—the intention to meet, listen, share, and learn from one another.

BEYOND THE DOCTRINE: THE FREEDOM OF COMPANIONSHIP

In these spaces, we find something different than what we've experienced in the institutional Church. We find freedom—the freedom to explore our spiritual paths without the constraints of dogma. We find the courage to ask the questions that the Church might have silenced. We find the ability to honor the sacred in our own way, while still being a part of a larger, more inclusive spiritual family.

In these circles, we are free to be ourselves, whether that's someone seeking to understand the Divine in new ways or someone who is still questioning everything. We don't need to conform; we just need to be there for each other. When we show up with open hearts, we will be received with open arms, and we create a space where the Spirit can move freely, guiding us in ways we never imagined.

COMPANIONSHIP IN THE UNSEEN

One of the most beautiful truths I've discovered on this journey is that companionship doesn't end with death. Even after Charlene passed—and later, after Cooper was gone—I've continued to feel their presence. We are never truly alone. The bonds we form with those we love are not limited by time or space. They live on in the unseen, in the quiet places where love and memory still echo.

In meditation, I've felt Charlene beside me—her presence guiding me in ways I can't explain. In dreams, Cooper still walks beside me, reminding me that love is eternal. These are sacred companions. Though no longer visible, they continue to shape my spiritual path.

And I believe these unseen connections are not unique to

me. They exist for all of us, waiting to be recognized, honored, and cherished.

THE LIVING CHURCH: REIMAGINED

The Church, as we once knew it, was meant to be a living, breathing organism—a place where people came together to encounter the Divine in one another. But the true Church isn't confined to a building or an institution. It's found in the hearts of seekers, in conversations around a table, and in the quiet moments of shared meditation.

When we gather in search of truth, of God, and of honest companionship, we are the Church. We become the Body of Christ—living and breathing through our love for one another.

As we've seen, the hunger for spiritual companionship runs deep, and the need for meaningful connection cannot be overstated.

In the next chapter, we'll explore how to build spiritual communities that exist beyond traditional walls—communities rooted in authenticity, intention, and shared seeking. We'll look at what these new gatherings can look like, how they function, and how you can begin to create or find your own sacred circle. The Church may have left the building, but the Spirit has not. It is moving among us still—gathering us in new and beautiful ways.

AFFIRMATION

> *I am not alone on this journey.*
> *God walks with me,*
> *and so do my companions,*
> *both seen and unseen.*

Together, we are the Body of Christ
—alive in love,
searching, growing, and discovering
the Divine in each other.

CHAPTER 10
BEYOND THE WALLS
A NEW KIND OF SPIRITUAL COMMUNITY

For most of my life, community had a familiar shape—built around pews, pulpits, and shared Sunday rhythms. But in the silence that followed Charlene's passing, I began to feel that shape no longer fit.

When I found myself alone in grief, I also found myself outside the Church—not by decision, but by silence. No call came from the Diocese. Though a chaplain is appointed to care for retired clergy, no one reached out—not with prayers, not with presence. From the institution I had faithfully served for over 35 years, there came only silence. And in that quiet, I realized just how far the Church had drifted from the heart of its mission.

As I began to talk with others, I discovered I wasn't alone. Many had felt that same quiet abandonment, particularly in moments of illness, loss, or transition. The Church we once turned to for comfort had become distant, even indifferent. We weren't longing for another sermon or service. We were aching for something sacred—something real, raw, and present—that could meet us in our brokenness without trying to fix us.

As I reflected on the Church's slow decline and its inability to offer that kind of presence, a question arose within me: Could true community exist beyond the church walls? Could spiritual connection thrive without stained glass, without clergy robes, without an order-of-service bulletin?

The answer came—unexpectedly—through COVID-19.

The pandemic disrupted everything we thought we knew about gathering. Sanctuaries closed, rituals paused, and even casual coffee hours disappeared. That disruption forced us to reimagine not just how we gathered but why. And in that strange vacuum, something surprising happened: people began finding God in unexpected places.

Families rediscovered meaning around Sunday brunch tables, where conversations about life and faith unfolded over waffles and coffee. Friends met for lunch and found themselves talking about God—without scripts, shame, or the need for formal prayers.

One of the most beautiful expressions of this new kind of fellowship happened in a local pub. We called it Theology on Tap. There were no dress codes. No organ preludes. No offering plates. Sometimes it was a priest. Other times, a thoughtful layperson. But always, it was real.

There was no pressure to believe a certain way—only an invitation to reflect, speak, and listen. And in that openness, something sacred emerged. What I witnessed in those gatherings was what the Church once offered at its best: connection, not just between people but between people and the Divine. These new forms of fellowship—whether over brunch, coffee, or a cold beer—were small, informal, and deeply human. And maybe that's precisely why they worked.

They reminded me that the community doesn't need walls. It needs honesty, compassion, space for laughter, questions, and quiet moments of silence, and, more than anything, presence. God was there, not in the grandeur of ritual, but in the calm simplicity of being together.

This wasn't confined to pubs or brunch spots. I began to see spiritual communities spring up in the most unlikely places—parks, living rooms, back patios, and even online.

A small group of friends I know began meeting once a week on a waterfront bench. They brought lawn chairs, thermoses of coffee, and open hearts. Sometimes, they read a passage from a book that stirred something spiritual. Other times, they sat in silence, soaking in God's presence reflected in the sea. Week after week, a sacred rhythm formed—one that held space for vulnerability and truth.

In another town, a couple began opening their home once a month for a simple potluck. It started with just a few friends and grew by word of mouth. They'd light a candle, say a few words of gratitude, and let the evening unfold. Conversations drifted between God, family, and purpose. But always, it came back to this: a longing to connect—to feel seen, heard, and loved.

Even in the digital world, where screens often divide us, spiritual communities have taken root. During the pandemic, many of us discovered the surprising intimacy of a Zoom screen. I've joined virtual gatherings with people from across states and countries who share prayers, meditation, and reflections on spiritual texts. These connections, while screen-bound, are no less real. In fact, for some, it's the only space where they feel truly seen.

What ties these gatherings together isn't theology or doctrine—it's intention. A shared hunger for something authentic and honest, free of performance. People show up as they are. There's room for doubt, laughter, and tears. And in that raw simplicity, the sacred is alive and well.

I've come to believe this is the future of spiritual community—not in grand sanctuaries or formal liturgies, but in kitchens and courtyards, on park benches and Zoom calls, over meals and music, and moments of honest reflection.

In these moments, I'm reminded that Jesus never built a cathedral. He gathered with people on hillsides, in homes, around tables. He broke bread. He told stories. He listened. Maybe what we need now isn't more church but more communion—not more institutions but more intimate circles of truth, compassion, and presence.

As the spiritual community expands beyond traditional walls, a quiet invitation remains: to carry that sacred connection inward. Part II has explored the outward journey—breaking free from institutional structures and rediscovering presence in living rooms, pubs, and unassuming moments of grace.

But the path does not end there. Beyond the gathering lies the deeper invitation: to live what we've found, not just to speak of grace but to embody it, not just to awaken but to walk awake.

In Part III, we enter the terrain where spiritual insight becomes spiritual practice, where belief is tested, refined, and —if we're willing—transformed. This is the inward unfolding.

AFFIRMATION

I am part of a sacred circle that needs no walls.
Wherever two or more gather in honesty and love,
Spirit is alive. I carry the light of community within me—
And I trust that the Divine meets us
wherever we dare to show up real.

PART THREE
WALKING THE PATH WITH DEPTH AND COURAGE

"You will know the truth, and the truth will make you free."
—John 8:32

There comes a time in every seeker's life when inspiration must become action—when the truths we've glimpsed in prayer, silence, and sacred longing begin to manifest in how we live, speak, love, and endure..

This is not the easy part of the journey. It is the point where faith becomes real—where we're challenged to move forward not by what we see but by a deeper trust that lives within the soul. To walk the spiritual path with depth and courage is to hold life's tensions: joy and grief, certainty and doubt, hope and heartbreak. It means letting our spiritual insights move beyond comforting ideas into lived practices—presence, compassion, and resilience. At this point, spirituality is no longer a retreat from life but a way of being fully present within it.

This part of the book is for the moments when the path feels unclear, or when the world asks more of us than we think we can give. It's about the everyday courage of choosing love when anger would be easier, staying present when it's tempting to be aloof, and continuing to seek even when God feels distant.

You don't need to be fearless to walk this path. You only need to be willing. Willing to show up. To trust the wisdom that's unfolding within you. And to believe that even on the hardest days, the Divine walks with you, as close as your breath.

Let us walk forward together—honest, human, and unafraid to go deep.

CHAPTER 11
THE INNER SELF AS TEACHER

As we begin this third part of the journey, we move from reflecting on the Church's fading influence, experiences of loss, and the mystical thread woven through our faith, into a deeper engagement with personal wisdom and spiritual courage. Here, we explore the Inner Self as not only a companion but also a guide, giving us a sacred strength found within and guiding us to discover the courage to trust our own inner knowing—the quiet, resilient voice of the soul.

In my earliest days of faith, I was taught to seek guidance from those who knew better—priests, theologians, and the grand tradition of the Church. And for a time, that served me well. The liturgy gave my prayers a rhythm, the community gave my soul a home, and the teachings gave my mind something to think about.

But beneath the words and forms, something quieter stirred —something more intimate, more inward. I now know it as life's greatest teacher: the Inner Self.

FROM DEPENDENCY TO DISCERNMENT

In most spiritual journeys, there comes a time when external structures feel essential. They offer safety, companionship, and a sense of direction—especially for those emerging from trauma or uncertainty. The rules feel like a lifeline. Eventually, however, these outer forms can begin to feel less like guidance and more like confinement. The soul no longer longs for safety—it yearns for authenticity. It seeks truth, not only in sermons or scripture, but in the stillness where spirit and self meet.

Many, like myself, leave the Church at this threshold—not out of rebellion, but because they are being drawn toward a more intimate knowledge of the Divine. The forms they once knew no longer hold the mystery. The hierarchy no longer inspires. The answers sound too rehearsed. And somewhere in the silence, a new voice begins to rise—the voice of the Inner Teacher.

It doesn't shout. It rarely argues. It often emerges in solitude—in grief, in beauty, in stillness. It is not the ego's chatter, but the soul's steady whisper—the place where Divine knowing and personal truth meet. It speaks not in commands but with quiet conviction. Not with dogma, but with deep knowing. This is the voice of the Spirit within—what Jesus called the Advocate or Comforter, and what mystics across the ages have named the Divine Spark, the Inner Light, the Indwelling Presence.

INTUITION AND THE HOLY SPIRIT

Traditional religion sometimes dismisses this inner voice as mere emotion or pride. But intuition is not impulse. It is the deep current beneath the surface waves of thought. It arises when the mind grows quiet and the heart opens. It speaks in images, hunches, sudden clarity, or a peaceful assurance that bypasses explanation. It rarely justifies itself. But it reveals itself in the fruit it bears.

What many call the Holy Spirit is deeply intuitive. It doesn't lecture—it moves through us like wind in the trees. Sometimes it stirs us with urgency; other times, it gently calms and brings peace. Trusting your intuition is often the same as trusting the Holy Spirit. God speaks quietly, but only when we are ready to listen. This doesn't mean discarding the wisdom of others, but it does mean we stop outsourcing our soul. We begin to test what we hear, not by creeds or consensus, but by the inner resonance of truth. Truth rings clear. Even when it calls us to something difficult, it does so without shame or fear.

THE COURAGE TO TRUST YOURSELF

We have often been taught that trusting ourselves is prideful or dangerous, but what if the deeper danger is abandoning the voice God planted within us?" Moving from spiritual dependency to inner guidance takes courage. It is far easier to follow rules than to listen inwardly. Rules are tidy. Intuition invites us into the unknown. It asks us to step into the fog and trust that the path will appear.

And yet, every great spiritual teacher has walked this very way. Jesus withdrew from the synagogue and the structures of power to pray alone, to listen inwardly, to follow divine instinct rather than public opinion. He said, "I do nothing on my own but speak just what the Father has taught me" (John 8:28).

And how did he learn? By intuition—in the hush of the desert, in the ache of solitude, and in communion with the Spirit—far from the noise of institutional voices..

Mystics have long pointed us inward, insisting that God is found not in institutions, but in the soul's quiet depths. Meister Eckhart faced opposition for saying so. Julian of Norwich received her vision not through church authority, but inner revelation.

Thomas Merton, whose writings shaped much of my own journey, once wrote:

> "At the center of our being is a point of nothingness... a point untouched by sin and by illusion, a point of pure truth... which belongs entirely to God."

Modern guides like Howard Thurman and Cynthia Bourgeault carry this same message forward: that God still speaks through silence, intuition, and the sacred voice within.

FROM GUIDANCE TO COMMUNION

There is a tenderness in this inward journey. No longer ruled by guilt or the need for approval, the soul begins to unfold. We receive the wisdom of tradition and learn to integrate it with our own discernment.

We no longer come to God as outsiders seeking permission. We realize God is already here—within us—inviting us to listen, to co-create, and to live from love.

I've lived long enough to know that external religion can fail us through silence, loss, or the hypocrisy of those we trusted. But the Inner Teacher never fails. When I was at my lowest—when I had no words to pray, and even the Church stood silent after Charlene died—it was this presence, this whispering Spirit, that remained.

This is the gift of the Inner Self: to lead us from belief into knowing, from dependence into authority, from fear into freedom. So I say to you, as one who has spent decades within the Church and now walks beyond its walls: You are not alone. You do not need a priest to hear God. You do not need permission to trust what stirs in your soul. The Spirit within you is real, alive, and wise. Listen. Follow. Trust. You are already walking with the Teacher—You. Your Inner Self

As we learn to trust the quiet wisdom of the Inner Self, something begins to shift. The journey becomes less about arriving at fixed beliefs and more about living into mystery. The soul, once tethered to outer authorities, is now drawn toward deeper waters—toward questions that transform us rather than answers that settle us. This is the beginning of a sacred pilgrimage, not of the feet, but of the spirit. In the next chapter, we step into that deeper journey—the Pilgrimage of the Soul—where inner trust becomes movement, and the way forward is shaped not by certainty, but by sacred unfolding.

AFFIRMATION

The wisdom I seek is already within me.
I listen with trust, and I follow with courage.

CHAPTER 12
PILGRIMAGE OF THE SOUL

We are all on a journey—not one marked by dogma or rigid beliefs, but a pilgrimage of the soul. Life itself is sacred ground, a sacred path we walk, and each step offers a chance to awaken, to grow, and to return to the Source from which we came.

No one is handed a roadmap at birth. Instead, we receive a beating heart, a questioning mind, and a soul that longs to remember its purpose. That longing is the first whisper of pilgrimage. It may come in a moment of joy—a sunrise cracking open the sky with light. Or it may rise out of pain, a deep sorrow that unsettles the soul and stirs the desire for something more.

My own pilgrimage has been shaped not by certainty but by the mystery of life in its moment, through time, love, grief, and grace. I've come to see that the truest spiritual path is not paved in theological precision but walked in openness, trust, and a willingness to be transformed by life itself.

THE PHYSICAL JOURNEY

At times, the soul's journey becomes undeniably physical. Illness, aging, the feel of bare feet on soil, or the simplicity of kneeling to tend a garden can awaken something profound and sacred within us. These often-overlooked experiences aren't separate from our spiritual lives—they're at the heart of them, moments where body and spirit meet, and something sacred is revealed.

I remember how grief left its imprint on my physical body—the heaviness in my limbs, the fatigue that no sleep could cure, the ache in my chest. I would instinctively reach for Charlene or Cooper, only to find empty space. And yet, even in those hollowed-out moments, something quietly stirred—a tenderness, a new sensitivity, a strange sense of presence in absence. These weren't beliefs to be taught, but quiet truths that lived in my body—truths I felt in my bones, whispers of the sacred in the silence of absence, in the midst of sorrow.

THE EMOTIONAL TERRAIN

Every pilgrim must travel through emotional valleys. This landscape can be jagged and unpredictable. We grieve, we yearn, we stumble, and we rise. Through all this, I've come to understand that our emotions are not deviations from the sacred journey—they are an integral part of it. They are not detours, but signposts—guiding us deeper into the truth of who we are and what we're becoming..

I've wept wordlessly in prayer. I've laughed out loud when joy slipped through the cracks of sorrow. And I've sat in silence, feeling lost and found in the same breath. Emotional honesty, in all its rawness, asks only that we bring our whole selves to the road we travel. It shapes us in ways belief never could.

SPIRITUAL AWAKENINGS ALONG THE WAY

Spiritual awakenings are rarely dramatic. More often, they arrive like a whisper or a change in the wind. They come in quiet spaces—dreams, silence, stillness, moments in nature. Sometimes they emerge in the middle of despair, when God seems distant, but something in us keeps reaching.

I've come to trust these awakenings, both subtle and profound. They don't always make sense in the moment. But looking back, I see how they opened me—gently or abruptly—to deeper truths. Some have come like fire—blazing, urgent, unmistakable. Others have been like water—soft, persistent, reshaping me without force.

The soul's deepest desire is to return to the Divine, and every awakening, no matter how small, is a step in that return.

SACRED PLACES, DIVINE ENCOUNTERS

Every pilgrimage has its holy ground, but these places are not always grand cathedrals or ancient shrines. They can be gardens blooming in spring, the hush of early morning by the water, or a hospital room heavy with love and silence. These are places where the veil feels thin, and something eternal stirs.

Often, we pass these sacred spaces without naming them. But looking back, we realize that the sacred had already found us. They become markers—memorial stones—on our spiritual map. They remind us that the ground we walk is holy, not because of where it is but because of how we walk it: with reverence, hope, and a heart cracked open by loss or joy.

Just as there are sacred places, there are sacred people. Some stay for a chapter, others for a lifetime. But each one, in their way, shifts something in us. I think of an artist friend who helped me see grief as a form of art, a stranger who shared a life-changing word, and a spiritual companion who asked the question that unraveled my certainties.

These are not random events. They are divine appointments—a phone call at just the right moment, a dream before the need arises, a line of poetry that feels like it was written just for you. Divine timing, I've learned, is never accidental. It's a golden thread that weaves the pilgrimage together, showing us that even when we feel lost, we are being guided, not by doctrine but the Living Mystery.

THE JOURNEY OVER DOCTRINE

Sacred moments defy description. They cannot be captured in bullet points or fit neatly into theological boxes. They must be lived. Perhaps this is why the soul's journey matters more than recited words—because we meet the Divine not in formulas, but in the unfolding of experience.

Doctrine never prepared me for the luminous presence in a hospital room or the way grief could soften my heart. The journey did. The journey still does. And I believe it always will. It teaches me to watch, to listen, to allow myself to be moved by the Divine—however, and wherever, it appears.

I've come to see God not just in scripture or sacrament, but in everything—in the quiet of early morning, in the smile of a stranger, in a song that opens the soul. These are the altars of the everyday. These are the places where faith is born anew. Too often, religion has traded wonder for certainty. But the soul does not thrive in cages. It blossoms in mystery. It grows in freedom—the freedom to question, to fall, to rise again, to walk the winding road with courage and trust.

Letting go of rigid belief didn't weaken my faith—it deepened it. It cleared the way for the real pilgrimage to begin: a journey not built on dogma but rooted in discovery. I am not chasing answers but receiving what is holy. I am not bound by belief but moved by love. I am not about arriving but walking with God beside me, every step of the way.

This is the pilgrimage of the soul. The soul must make a brave choice to release the need to know and embrace the courage to trust. Letting go of certainty doesn't mean losing faith—it means making room for something more alive, immediate, and real. It means walking with open hands instead of clenched fists. It means trusting that not having all the answers can still lead to wisdom. It means finding God not in clarity but in communion.

This next chapter invites us to loosen our grip on certainties —religious, personal, even spiritual—and discover what grace can only reveal when we stop demanding to understand.

AFFIRMATION

I trust my soul's pilgrimage,
knowing that each step is sacred.
I embrace the journey, surrendering certainty
and walking with love, faith, and openness.

CHAPTER 13
LETTING GO OF CERTAINTY

Certainty is a comfortable companion. It gives us answers to cling to, rules to follow, and a sense of control in an often unpredictable world. It tells us we're right, safe, and on the "correct" path. In my early walk with God, I held onto certainty like a lifeline. Scripture said it, the Church affirmed it, and I believed my faith rested securely in the answers I was given.

But as my relationship with God deepened, I began to notice that certainty often came at a cost. Over time, it began to feel less like a foundation and more like a fence. This fence wrapped itself around wonder, offering quick answers when my soul truly needed time, space, silence, and room to breathe. The questions I once feared began to feel like sacred invitations—not to solve a puzzle but to step into a mystery.

To live spiritually beyond the Church is not simply to walk away from tradition—it is to step into a space where God is no longer fenced in by answers. It is to welcome a faith that thrives not in knowing everything, but in trusting deeply—even when we know very little.

THE MYSTERY AT THE HEART OF GOD

God is not a riddle to be solved. God is mystery, depth, and presence. The spiritual life is not about collecting beliefs like artifacts—it's about communion. Some of the holiest moments in my life were not when I understood something new but when I surrendered the need to understand at all.

When Charlene died, the questions came like a flood. Where was God? Why do prayers go unanswered? Why must love and loss be so intertwined? I didn't find satisfying answers. But I did find something else—an aching stillness, a strange peace that settled beneath the storm.

Not knowledge. But knowing.

And through it all, there was never a doubt in our hearts that God was with us. Even amid grief, even as we faced the unknown, there was a quiet assurance that we were not alone —not because we understood the mystery but because we felt held within it. There were no divine explanations handed down, no voice from the heavens with reasons why. But there was Presence—steady, unshakable, and deeply real.

I want you to hear that, especially if you're standing in the fog of doubt or sorrow: being faithful doesn't mean having it all figured out. Faith is not the absence of questions. It's the willingness to stay open, even when the answers don't come. It's trusting that God is not distant from your doubt but woven into it, closer than breath.

You may never find the reason why. Life may never make complete sense. But that doesn't mean God is absent. God is not an answer, but a Presence. And that Presence will meet you in your confusion, aching, and silence. It met Charlene and me in ours. And I believe it will meet you, too.

That is the difference: Certainty seeks to define God. Communion lets God define us.

THE COURAGE TO NOT KNOW

We've been trained to equate doubt with weakness and ambiguity with failure. But the opposite is often true. It takes real courage to walk through questions without demanding answers. It takes faith to admit "I don't know" and trust that God is near.

In fact, many of the truest things I believe are not things I can prove—they're things I've come to know in the quiet chambers of the soul.

The Church often offered me doctrines to believe, creeds to recite, and lines to memorize. But the deeper truths of my life came not from the pulpit but from the pauses in between—from dreams, from nature, from weeping in the dark and still finding grace in the morning.

Faith, I've come to learn, is not about being sure. It's about being open. It is not the absence of doubt—it is the decision to keep walking with God even when the way is unclear.

HOLY SPACE IS NOT EMPTY

Some fear that when we let go of certainty, we fall into a spiritual void. But I've found the opposite. The space that opens up is not a vacuum—it is holy. It is full of Presence, complete with possibility; it is the place where the Spirit moves.

Too often, the Church rushed to fill this space with doctrine and answers, afraid that emptiness might imply absence. But I've learned: we don't always need to fill that space with words. Sometimes, awe is enough. Silence is enough. Breath is enough. There is a knowing deeper than thought—a truth that reveals itself not through logic but through love.

Mystics across the ages have spoken of the "cloud of unknowing," the divine darkness, the luminous void. These are not places of abandonment but of encounter. They are where we lay down the idols of certainty and kneel before God, who is always more than we imagined.

A NEW KIND OF FAITH

I no longer need to be certain. I need only to be faithful. That means showing up, listening, and trusting what rings true in the stillness of my being. Faith is not a set of beliefs to defend—it's a relationship to be lived and experienced. One that moves gently between certainty and doubt, deepens in wonder, and unfolds with the changing seasons of the soul.

I've come to believe that the purpose of faith is not to give us control, but to invite us into connection, not to hand us a script, but to teach us how to improvise with love.

So I offer you this:

Sometimes, the deepest truth isn't found in what we can explain, but in what we're willing to understand and embrace. And if you find yourself sitting in the dark, not with answers, but with an open hand, waiting—that, too, is faith. That is the surrender of certainty. And yes—that, too, is God. For even in the silence, the mystery speaks.

When we let go of certainty, we open ourselves to a deeper, unspoken knowing—the kind found in moments when the world falls away and we encounter the Divine. These are the "thin places," where time bends, and we feel God's presence in the quiet spaces between breaths. In these sacred moments, the need for answers fades, and we are simply with the Divine, held in timeless grace.

In the next chapter, we explore these holy places where mystery unfolds, and the ordinary becomes extraordinary, where faith is less about knowing and more about being present to the mystery that surrounds us.

AFFIRMATION

I do not need all the answers to walk in faith.
I let go of certainty and open my heart to mystery.
God meets me not in what I know,
but in the trust that carries me forward.

CHAPTER 14
THIN PLACES AND TIMELESS MOMENTS

There are places and moments when the world grows transparent—not just beautiful or quiet, but translucent—where the ordinary thins and something vast, eternal, and unnamed presses close. You do not see it with your eyes. You feel it, like the breath of God moving through the veil.

These are the thin places the Celts spoke of—where heaven and earth seem to touch. But I have found they are not limited to mountaintops or ancient stone chapels. They can be found in the sigh of wind through trees, in the hush between a loved one's final breath and the silence that follows, or in the deep stillness of meditation when the self dissolves and only Presence remains.

In these moments, time doesn't just slow—it disappears. There is only now. The ticking clock fades into irrelevance. You are nowhere and everywhere at once. The veil parts, and eternity spills in like light through a door cracked open.

I've known these timeless moments in dreams, where the dead returned not as memories but as luminous beings of love and wisdom. I've touched them in prayer, when I was not speaking to God but with God—no longer separate, no longer afraid. I've entered them in meditation, where stillness became a doorway, and presence arrived without words. And I've walked them in nature, where a tree stood not as wood and leaf, but as a living icon of the Holy. I remember a quiet dawn at the edge of a lake, when the mist curled like incense and the world seemed to exhale holiness. I recall a moment in grief when, shattered by loss, I felt not despair but a profound sense of being held by something unseen and eternal.

These are not just poetic metaphors. They are real, more real than the concrete certainties the Church once demanded I cling to. In these experiences, I don't need doctrine. I am known. I am loved. I am home.

Mystics have tried to speak of such moments for centuries. Julian of Norwich described seeing in her hand something the size of a hazelnut, and hearing the words, "It is all that is made." She heard Christ say, "All shall be well, and all shall be well, and all manner of thing shall be well." Meister Eckhart, who said, "The eye with which I see God is the eye with which God sees me." John of the Cross described the soul's journey through the "dark night," only to awaken into the divine embrace. Teresa of Ávila, in ecstasy, wrote of her soul being pierced by God's love, an experience so intense and intimate that she struggled for words.

Thomas Merton stood at the corner of Fourth and Walnut in Louisville, Kentucky, and felt a sudden clarity: that all people were shining like the sun, if only we could see it. His vision was one of unity, of heaven breaking through the mundane.

These are voices from the edge of the veil, trying to put into language what is beyond language. They remind us that the veil grows thin not only in monasteries or on mountaintops, but also wherever the human heart is quiet enough to listen, wait, and truly see.

You don't have to chase these experiences. They reveal themselves when the soul is open, often when we least expect them: in times of grief and awe, in surrender, in the pause between breaths, in the letting go of control. It is the trust that the Divine still speaks, appears, and breaks through the veil in flashes of timeless grace. All we need is the courage to listen—and the willingness to be changed.

As we journey through these thin places, where time and eternity intertwine, we realize that we are not walking alone. The Divine meets us in these sacred moments, but we also find companions along the way—those who walk beside us, sharing the road, the silence, and the mystery. In our next chapter, we reflect on the importance of these companions, whether in the form of kindred spirits, guides, or the quiet presence of God, and how, together, we continue the journey of faith, even without the structure of the Church. This final word is a reminder that no matter how solitary our path may feel, we are never truly alone.

AFFIRMATION

I trust that the Divine is always near,
speaking to me through thin places and timeless moments.
I am open to the grace that appears when I least expect it,
and I welcome the sacred in the ordinary.

CHAPTER 15
COMPANIONS ON THE ROAD

Many people fear leaving the Church because they wonder, "Where do I go from here?" Without a pulpit, creed, or common prayer to lean on, the spiritual path can feel untethered—and yet, it can also feel more alive than ever. The absence of boundaries becomes a doorway to something richer, something deeper. This chapter is about finding security in knowing you are not the first to step through that doorway.

As I have shared, my journey beyond the Church did not mean abandoning Jesus. On the contrary, it deepened my reverence for him as an anointed teacher, a Christed being whose message was not about exclusivity but universality. Jesus spoke of the Kingdom of Heaven within, of unity with the Father, of loving one another as ourselves. These teachings are not the property of Christianity alone. They resonate across the globe and throughout history, echoed in the voices of mystics, prophets, and sages from many ancient traditions.

A quote attributed to Thomas Merton, the Trappist monk and contemplative, reads: "If you want to identify me, ask me not where I live or what I like to eat, but ask me what I am living for." This sentiment captures a truth Merton embodied. Though rooted in Catholicism, he drew deeply from Eastern philosophy and interfaith dialogue. He understood what many mystics have discovered: that Truth is not confined to a single path. It reveals itself in stillness, in service, in love.

Rumi, the 13th-century Sufi poet, wrote in his poem "A Great Wagon": "Out beyond ideas of wrongdoing and rightdoing, there is a field. I'll meet you there." In that field, there is no doctrine, no dogma—only presence. Rumi's words dance with the same Spirit I have felt in prayer, in grief, and in dreams. Like Jesus, he invites us beyond the mind's divisions into the heart's wholeness.

Yogananda, the Indian yogi who brought the science of Kriya Yoga to the West, taught that "the soul loves to meditate, for in contact with the Spirit lies its greatest joy." Meditation continued to be an anchor after I lost both Charlene and Cooper. It allowed me to move from theological ideas about God to a lived experience of the Divine. In that silence, I found companionship not only with my beloved but with saints and sages I had never met.

Mystics have always been the spiritual rebels—those who challenged the institutions of their time because they encountered God directly. Julian of Norwich, Meister Eckhart, Hildegard of Bingen, Teresa of Ávila: they did not need permission to speak of their visions. Their authority came from within. So does yours. To walk a spiritual path is not to adopt a new belief system. It is to listen, observe, and live with curiosity and reverence. Read widely, listen deeply, and let your heart be your tuning fork. If something resonates as true, it likely carries the ring of Spirit.

Edgar Cayce, often called the sleeping prophet, once said: "Spirit is the Life, Mind is the Builder, and the Physical is the Result." That simple framework reshaped my understanding of creation. It affirmed that we are not separate from the Divine but part of it—co-creators within its unfolding mystery.

The Law of One, a channeled body of work that deeply impacted me, says: "All things, all of life, all of the creation is part of one original thought." There is no outside of God. No us and them. No saved and unsaved. Just One. And within that Oneness, an infinite variety of paths, personalities, and ways of seeking.

You may find the Divine in a cathedral or a cave, a synagogue or a sunset. What matters is not the form, but the awareness—that you are present, that you are listening, that you are willing to love.

As you move beyond the walls of the Church, know this: you are not alone. You walk among mystics, teachers, and pilgrims who have always followed the wider stream. Some wore robes. Some carried staffs. Others wrote poems or channeled visions. But all of them, in their way, remind us that the Spirit blows where it will.

And it has not stopped speaking.

AFFIRMATION

I walk this path with an open hand and an open heart.
I am part of the One, and the One is part of me.
The same Spirit that breathed through
Jesus, Rumi, Julian, and the sages of old,
breathes through me now.
I do not fear the wide horizon,
for love is my compass and God is my home.
I walk among companions seen and unseen,
and every step of the way is guided by the Eternal.

PART FOUR
BLESSINGS AND PRACTICES FOR THE JOURNEY

BLESSINGS ON THE ROAD AHEAD

As you step forward, remember: the spiritual life is not meant to be a solitary climb up a distant mountain. It is a shared meal, a meaningful glance, a conversation that opens the heart. You don't need a cathedral to find the holy. Sometimes, all it takes is a coffee cup, a candle, and a listening ear. So...

- Go have brunch with your family.
- Meet an old friend for lunch and talk about the real stuff.
- Light a candle with a few companions and let the Spirit speak through silence, prayer, and shared stories.
- Join others at a local pub—yes, have a beer on tap— and talk honestly about the things that matter: love, loss, longing, and the mystery of God.

This is the Church, too. It is communion, companionship,

and what mystics call Spirit in motion. Let your spiritual practice be alive, with joy and honest conversation. Let your faith be embodied in laughter, kindness, and courage. And when the way feels uncertain, return to what grounds you: breath, stillness, beauty, and community. You are not alone. Others are finding their way, too.

Keep walking.
Keep reaching.
Keep showing up—heart open, soul awake.

FINAL WORD

We have walked together through memories and moments of disillusionment, grief, awakening, and rediscovery. We've explored what it means to find God not within stone walls or stained glass, but in silence, solitude, friendship, the natural world, dreams, loss, and love. This journey has not been linear, and it hasn't always been easy. But perhaps that is the mark of any spiritual path worth walking—it winds, it deepens, and it asks more of us than passive belief. It calls us to presence, to courage, to love.

If you've ever felt abandoned by the Church, take heart. You have not been abandoned by God.

The institution may have failed to see your soul, but the Divine never has.

You are already deeply known and deeply loved.

That truth is not reserved for pews and pulpits—it rises with the sun, lives in the rhythm of your breath, and whispers in the quiet moments when you are most yourself.

I hope you've found something in these pages to accompany you along the way. May you return to them as needed, for this journey—this finding of God beyond the Church—is not a destination, but an unfolding path. Step by step, it prepares you for what lies ahead. And through it all, remember this: the sacred has been walking with you all along.

A SENDING BLESSING

May you go in peace,
not because all the answers are clear,
but because you have learned to live
in the beauty of the questions.
May your table be full of food and friendship.
May your days include sacred pauses—
a candlelit gathering, a moment of shared silence,
a story told over coffee or a beer.
May your laughter echo through the heavens,
and your tears be caught by the One who holds all things.
May you find God not only in prayer,
but in the clink of glasses, the warmth of bread,
the kindness of strangers, and the embrace of friends.
And when the road ahead is winding and strange,
may love be your compass,
and may your soul remember this truth:
You are home—right here, right now—
each time you choose to be fully present.
Amen. And so it is.

PRACTICES FOR THE JOURNEY

Before we part, I want to leave you with more than words. What follows is a collection of practices and reflections—a mystical toolbox gathered from my own journey—that you can carry with you. Think of this not as a rulebook but as a field guide—a companion for quiet mornings, restless nights, and moments when your soul aches for something more.

Use what serves you. Leave what doesn't. Return whenever you need to remember that the sacred is not far away. It's right here—in breath, in silence, in longing, in love. These practices are not the way. They are simply a way, offered humbly, from one seeker to another. So open your heart. Try something new. Or reclaim something ancient you forgot you loved. And let the Spirit meet you there.

1. STILLNESS: ENTERING THE INNER SANCTUARY

Mystics through the ages have known: silence is not the absence of sound but the presence of God. Meditation is not about escaping the world, but descending into it—through the heart's doorway, into the chamber of the Divine.

- Use sacred words, gentle breath, or focused awareness to sink into stillness.
- Let thoughts come and go like clouds in a vast sky.
- Sit not to "achieve" but to be met.
- In the silence, something eternal speaks.

2. SACRED IMAGINATION: MEETING THE DIVINE IN INNER WORLDS

Imagination is not fantasy—it is the soul's canvas. Sacred imagination awakens spiritual sight, allowing you to walk alongside Christ, speak with your soul's guide, or relive a memory touched by Grace.

- In prayer or meditation, step into a sacred story—biblical or personal.
- Sense the surroundings. Feel the presence.
- Let the moment unfold as a living encounter, not a performance.
- Ask, listen, receive. The spirit speaks in image and feeling.

3. SACRED READING: HEARING THE VOICE BETWEEN THE LINES

Let every true word be Scripture. When your soul is open, the Divine speaks through poetry, prose, and even a stranger's sentence overheard. In this reimagined lectio divina, we become listeners of the Mystery hidden in plain sight.

- Choose a text that stirs your spirit—ancient or modern.
- Let a word rise, shimmer, and draw you inward.
- Breathe with it. Listen with the heart.
- Let it become prayer—alive and reciprocal.

4. NATURE AS TEMPLE: WALKING INTO THE INFINITE

The earth is the first cathedral, the sky its dome, the wind its chant. When organized religion fails, the wild holiness of nature remains—untamed, unfiltered, unmistakably sacred.

- Walk slowly. Let your senses be your prayer.
- Touch bark. Taste silence. Greet the moon.
- Speak aloud or in the heart. Then listen—trees speak in patience, rivers in rhythm.
- Let the Creator come to you not as sermon, but as scent and breeze.

5. DREAMWORK: OPENING THE GATEWAYS OF THE SOUL

Dreams are more than echoes of the mind—they are sacred doorways. In the silence of night, the veil grows thin. Messages, symbols, and encounters arrive not randomly, but as soul-whispers—gifts from the Divine and your higher self.

- View your dreams as sacred scripture written in the ink of the unconscious.
- Ask: What mystery seeks to be known? What part of me longs to awaken?
- Record without judgment. Interpret with awe. Trust the symbols—they belong to your soul.

THE MYSTICAL TOOLBOX
MEDITATIONS FOR ENCOUNTERING THE DIVINE

I would like to begin with what has recently become my favorite meditation, introduced to me by author John Mabry. It is a beautiful practice that draws from both shamanic and Christian mystical traditions. Often called spiritual journeying, it invites us into a sacred inner landscape — in this case, Jesus' carpentry shop — as a soul-safe, symbol-rich space to commune with the Divine.

This approach echoes the spirituality of saints like Ignatius of Loyola, who urged followers not merely to read about Jesus but to walk beside him in imagination — to sit with him, work with him, and experience his presence as real and transformative.

In shamanic language, such inner spaces become power places, where wisdom and healing can be received. Jesus's carpentry shop is especially powerful — a space of creation and repair, quiet companionship, and unconditional love.

Sitting with Jesus not as a distant deity but as a brother, teacher, and guide is profoundly healing. This is the true purpose of these practices: not theology, but transformation.

1. MEDITATION: IN THE CARPENTRY SHOP OF JESUS

(This one is my favorite.)

Begin by finding a quiet, comfortable space.
Sit or lie down. Close your eyes.
Let your breath slow and deepen...

Breathe in...and out.

Let the tension soften in your body.
Feel the weight of the day fall away like sawdust from a bench.

You are safe. You are loved.

Now imagine yourself walking down a dusty path
in a small village...

Stone homes nestled along a hillside...

Children playing in the street...
goats and laughter nearby...

And there—at the edge of town—
is a small wooden structure.
You recognize it as a carpentry shop.

The door is open.
The scent of wood and olive oil greets you.

And standing inside — his back to you — is Jesus.
He turns slowly.
His face lights up at the sight of you.

His eyes—so kind, so full of knowing—
meet yours with pure love.

He gestures with a smile to a nearby stool. You sit.
He sits beside you.

There are no words needed. Only presence.

Feel his love begin to surround you —
like warm sunlight on your skin...
like strong arms around your heart.

You are held in complete safety...

Nothing is required of you here.
You are enough.
Let yourself rest in that love.
Let it fill every part of you...
Clearing out worry...
Soothing old wounds...
Bringing peace to your soul.

Pause here. Stay as long as you wish in this quiet companionship.

When you're ready, Jesus may speak
—or simply gaze into your eyes.
He may place a hand on your shoulder or over your heart.

You are not alone. You never have been.
He smiles once more...
And you know this place will always be here.
Always open.
Always waiting.

Now, gently return to your breath...
Back to the room around you...
Carry this peace with you.
And when you're ready...open your eyes.

2. THE SACRED BREATH: A MEDITATION ON DIVINE PRESENCE

Find a quiet space where you can sit comfortably,
or lie down if that feels more restful.
Close your eyes and take a deep, slow breath in,
feeling the air fill your lungs,
then gently exhale,
releasing any tension or heaviness.
Let each breath you take bring you more deeply into stillness,
into this present moment.

Now, bring your awareness to your breath.
Notice the rhythm—
the way it enters your body,
and the way it leaves.

Breathing in, you are receiving the gift of life.
Breathing out, you are releasing all that no longer serves you.

With each inhale,
imagine you are drawing in light...warmth...love
...and the presence of the Divine.

With each exhale,
let go of any thoughts...fears...or worries.

Feel the sacredness of this simple, yet profound act—

breathing in and breathing out.

It is in this space of breath
that you are connected to the Divine,
present in every moment,
in every inhale and exhale.

As you continue to breathe,
imagine the breath is not only filling your body,
but also your heart...your mind...your soul.

Each breath becomes a doorway
to deeper connection with God,
a reminder of the infinite love that surrounds you.

Now, in the space between breaths,
feel the stillness.
This is the space where God dwells,
where presence is fully known.

Sit here for a moment, in the silence between breaths,
allowing yourself to simply be.

There is no need to rush.

There is nothing you need to do
but rest in the Divine presence
that fills the air around you...and within you.

Know that with every breath,
you are closer to the heart of the Creator.

You are held...you are loved...
you are a living vessel of the Divine.

When you are ready,
bring your awareness back to the present moment,
gently wiggling your fingers and toes.

Take a deep, refreshing breath in,
and as you exhale, slowly open your eyes,
carrying this quiet presence with you.

The Divine is in your breath,
and wherever you go,
God's presence goes with you.

3. MEDITATION ON THE NATURAL WORLD: A CONTEMPLATION WITH CREATION

Close your eyes and draw in a deep breath.
Feel the cool, living air enter your lungs.
Exhale slowly, releasing all tension, all distractions.

Again—
Inhale the breath of life.
Exhale and become still.

Now imagine yourself in a place of untouched beauty
—a forest at dawn, a hillside washed in sunlight,
the edge of the ocean under stars.
Wherever your soul feels most alive in nature,
go there now in your inner vision.

You walk slowly, reverently.
Each step is a prayer.
Each sound—a hymn.
Each breath—communion.

Notice how the earth beneath your feet welcomes you,
how the trees stand like ancient sentinels of silence.
The wind speaks not in words, but in wisdom.
The birds sing the original psalms.

You are not separate from this beauty.

You are part of it—flesh of the soil...breath of the wind...
spark of the same Divine fire that called all things into being.

Sit now beneath a tree, or beside a stream,
or upon a rock warmed by the sun.
Listen.
Listen not just with your ears, but with your spirit.
What is nature whispering to you today?

...pause...

Perhaps it is reminding you of your belonging...
Or showing you how to surrender,
like the leaf that falls in its time...
Or simply asking you to be—nothing more, nothing less.

Offer a wordless prayer of gratitude.
Feel your soul soften into this sacred belonging.
Let your heartbeat become the drumbeat of the Earth.
Let your breath rise and fall with the rhythm of the trees.
Let your thoughts drift like clouds across a spacious sky.

You are home.
You are holy.
And the natural world is a cathedral not built by hands.
Remain here as long as you wish.

And when you're ready, gently return.
Bring the stillness with you.
Let the world around you become your sanctuary,
the birds your choir, and the breeze your benediction.
You have touched the Divine in creation.
And it has touched you.

4. HEART-CENTERED MEDITATION: A RETURN TO THE SACRED WITHIN

Close your eyes.
Place a hand gently over your heart.
Feel the steady rhythm—
the pulse of life moving within you.

This is where the Sacred resides.
Not above...not beyond.
But here, within.

Take a deep breath in...
And release.
Again, slowly...
Inhale love.
Exhale peace.

Let your awareness settle into your chest.
Noticing the space behind your breastbone...

This is more than a beating muscle.
This is your soul's sanctuary—
A temple not built by human hands.

Within this heart-space, the Divine dwells—

Silent, luminous, ever-present.
It is the still point in your turning world.
The flame that never goes out.

Let your breath move in and out of this space.
With every inhale, draw in Divine Presence.
With every exhale, let go of all that is not love.

Now, gently ask:
Beloved within me, what do you wish to show me today?
Then listen.
Not with ears, but with the heart.

...*pause*...

Perhaps a word rises...or an image...
Or maybe just stillness—holy and enough.

Stay here.
Rest in this sanctuary.
Let love wash through you like light through stained glass.

If there are wounds here, cradle them in compassion.
If there is joy, let it bloom wide and wild.
If there is sorrow, let it be held, not fixed.

You are not alone.
You are not broken.
You are beloved.

Remain in this stillness as long as you like.
And when it feels right, slowly bring your awareness back.
Wiggle your fingers... your toes...
But leave the doorway to your heart open.

Carry this sacred awareness with you into your day.
Let your life become a prayer—
Each act an offering, each word a blessing.
For the Divine lives here.
And so do you.

5. CENTERING BREATH: A RETURN TO THE PRESENT MOMENT

Come to stillness...
Sit or stand with a tall spine.
Let your shoulders soften.
Let your jaw unclench.
Let your eyes gently close.

Place one hand on your belly.
The other is over your heart.
Feel the warmth of your touch.

Now, take a slow, deep breath in through your nose...
Feel your belly rise beneath your hand.
And exhale gently through your mouth...

Feel your body settle just a little more.
Again—
Inhale deeply...
And exhale fully.

With each breath, come home.
To this body.
To this moment.
To this breath.

Let your breath be an anchor—
A tether to the here and now.
Let the world's noise fall away.

Let yesterday rest in peace.
Let tomorrow wait its turn.

There is only this breath.
Only now.
And in this now,
God is here.
Breathing you.
Loving you.
Being you.

With every inhale, receive sacred Presence.
With every exhale, release resistance, worry, or striving.

You are not doing this alone.
The breath has always been with you—
Faithful, quiet, and holy.

Let it guide you inward.
To the still place beneath all doing.
Where you are enough.
Where the Holy whispers your name.

Breathe.
And be.

6. SACRED WALKING:
A PRACTICE OF MOVING WITH THE DIVINE

This is not a walk for exercise.
This is a walk for presence.
A walk for prayer.
A walk for meeting God along the way.

Find a quiet path—
a wooded trail, a sidewalk at dawn, a garden at dusk.

Stand still before you begin.
Feel your feet on the ground.
Let the earth hold you.

Take one slow, deep breath.
"Here I am."

Now begin to walk slowly.
Let your steps be gentle and mindful.

Let your breath find a rhythm with your movement.
Here... now... here... now...

Let your senses awaken.
What do you see?
What do you hear?
What stirs in your heart?

This path is holy ground.
The rustle of leaves, the cry of a bird, the sunlight on stone—
all of it speaks of the Sacred.

If thoughts arise, let them pass like clouds.
Return your attention to your feet, your breath, your surroundings.
What are you saying to me?

Walk until your heart feels quiet.
Walk until your soul feels heard.
And when you are ready to return, do so slowly.
With gratitude.
With awareness.
With reverence.

"Thank you. I was not alone."
Because you never are.
Each step is accompanied.
Each moment is infused with Presence.

7. EVENING RELEASE: A PRACTICE OF LETTING GO BEFORE SLEEP

The day is done.

Its beauty, its burdens,
its noise and its silence—
all of it has passed through you.
Now is the time to release.

Find a quiet space.
Dim the lights.
Light a candle if you wish.

Lie down or sit comfortably.

Place a hand over your heart or on your belly.
Feel the rise and fall of your breath.

Take three slow, deep breaths.
Inhale peace...
Exhale all that you no longer need.

Say gently to yourself: "I let go."
Let go of the need to fix.
Let go of the need to finish.
Let go of the voices of doubt,
the regrets, the replayed moments.
You do not need to carry it all into the night.

Imagine placing the weight of the day
into Divine hands.
You are held.
You are safe.
You are enough.

Now name three things from your day
for which you are grateful.
Whisper them like a blessing.
Then say: "This day is complete. I rest in God."

Close your eyes.
Let silence hold you.
Let the darkness be a soft cloak.

Let sleep come like grace.
And if dreams rise,
may they carry wisdom.
If memories stir, may they bring healing.

You are not alone.
You are not forgotten.
Even in sleep,
you are deeply loved.

8. SANCTUARY OF SOUND: A MEDITATION WITH MUSIC AND SPIRIT

(This is another of my favorites.)

Find a space where sound can surround you gently.
Play a piece of music that speaks to your soul—
instrumental, chant, classical, ambient—
whatever opens the heart.

Close your eyes.
Let the music wash over you like water.
Let it enter you not as sound alone,
but as Spirit.

Each note is a breath from the Divine.
Each vibration a whisper from the Beyond.

Feel where the music lands in your body:
Does a violin string tug at your heart?
Does a cello hum in your belly?
Does the piano echo in your bones?

Let it move you.
Let it stir what needs stirring.
Let it soothe what aches.

"Make me a sanctuary of sound."

Let each inhale open you wider.
Let each exhale dissolve resistance.

Let tears fall if they come.
Let joy rise if it will.

Let silence follow when the music ends—
sacred, pregnant, whole.

Remain in that silence.

Listen deeper still.
What do you hear in the quiet now?
A phrase?
A presence?
A peace?

Carry this soundless sound with you.
You are the sanctuary now.
Wherever you go,
the song continues.

9. DREAM GATE MEDITATION: A MYSTICAL ENCOUNTER BEYOND THE VEIL OF SLEEP

Find a comfortable position and begin to slow your breathing.
Let the weight of the day dissolve.
Feel your body anchored in this sacred moment.
Let your awareness descend,
like mist settling over a quiet meadow.

Inhale slowly...
Exhale fully...

Now imagine yourself walking barefoot along a twilight path.
The air is still.
The world hushed.
Around you, stars begin to shimmer
above trees that hold their breath.

Ahead, you see a gate—
ornate, ancient, made of light and mystery.
This is the Gate of Dreams—
a threshold between waking and soul-travel.

You know this place.
You've stood here before,
perhaps in childhood,
perhaps in sleep.

You approach it with reverence.
As you do, the gate begins to open—
not outward, but inward, into your deepest self.

Step through gently...

You now find yourself in a sacred garden of the soul.
Here, symbols live and speak.
Here, your guides walk with you, unseen but known.

Notice what is around you:
the colors, shapes, perhaps a sound or scent.
This is your personal dream realm—
woven from memory, meaning, and spirit.

In this space, you are not alone.

A luminous presence approaches—

perhaps an angel, a beloved soul, or your own higher self.
Feel no fear. Only love and wisdom dwell here.

Ask them: "What truth do I need to receive tonight?
What longing in me is ready to speak through dreams?"

Wait.
Listen with your heart.

...pause...

Now, slowly return.
Step back through the dream gate.
Know that when you sleep, you will re-enter this space.
You will dream with intention, with openness, and with trust.

You may wish to place a journal beside your bed.
When you awaken, write whatever you remember.
Even a word, a feeling, or an image is a seed from Spirit.

Let the gate remain open in your heart.
You are seen. You are guided.
And your dreams are a sacred conversation with the Divine.

However you choose to practice—whether walking in the woods, sitting in silence, or dreaming under starlight—know this: the sacred is not far off. It lives and moves within you. These practices are not meant to bind you, but to set you free. Try them. Adapt them. Let them evolve. And most of all, trust your soul's own way of drawing near to the Divine. Perhaps the greatest spiritual tool is the reminder that you are already a temple of the Divine. No institution can revoke what was written in your soul. Trust your longing. Trust your experience. Trust that the path, however lonely or winding, leads you back to the God who never left, and never will.

www.ingramcontent.com/pod-product-compliance
Lightning Source LLC
Chambersburg PA
CBHW031343160426
43196CB00007B/723